WRITING ON THE EDGE:
GREAT CONTEMPORARY WRITERS
ON THE FRONT LINE OF CRISIS

WRITING ON THE EDGE:
GREAT CONTEMPORARY WRITERS
ON THE FRONT LINE OF CRISIS

A Book by Tom Craig

Photography by Tom Craig / Edited by Dan Crowe

MARTIN AMIS

DANNY BOYLE

TRACY CHEVALIER

JIM CRACE

DANIEL DAY-LEWIS

MICHEL FABER

DAMON GALGUT

AA GILL

JOANNE HARRIS

HARI KUNZRU

ALI SMITH

JON MCGREGOR

DBC PIERRE

MINETTE WALTERS

New York · Paris · London · Milan

Published in association with Doctors Without Borders/Médecins Sans Frontières

First published in the United States of America in 2010
by Rizzoli International Publications, Inc.
300 Park Avenue South
New York, NY 10010
www.rizzoliusa.com

2010 2011 2012 / 10 9 8 7 6 5 4 3 2 1

Printed in China

Design by Studio8 Design

ISBN: 978-0-8478-3291-0

Library of Congress Cataloging-in-Publication Data

Writing on the edge : great contemporary writers on the front
line of crisis / Tom Craig [introduction] ; edited by Dan Crowe ;
essays by Martin Amis ... [et al.].
p. cm.
ISBN 978-0-8478-3291-0 (alk. paper)
1. Médecins sans frontières (Association) 2. Humanitarian
assistance--Developing countries. 3. Medical assistance--
Developing countries. 4. Disaster relief--Developing countries. 5.
War relief--Developing countries. I. Craig, Tom. II. Crowe, Dan.
RA390.F8W75 2010
808'.06661--dc22
2009044208

Captions by Tom Craig

Slugs in a Jar

I was in Liberia when I first likened my head to a glass jar. There were monkey arms on the grill and small, gun-toting boys who had little scars on their cheeks where grown men had made cuts and rubbed, with their dirty thumbs, amphetamines from some boat from Korea. It seemed that for every terrible thing I saw, one more slug would slide up into the jar, and when I went home to the warm fold of a posh pub in London, a few would slide out again. If the jar ever got full, that was it: I could never go home the same again.

The regularity of even the small atrocities is like a vibration. I knew I had to do something, no, try to do something. Squeak from my soapbox or wheeze from my window; I wanted to yell from the roof to everyone Euro-comfy that they must, at the very least, hear about the slugs.

I have no medical skills—in fact, no skills at all to help inventive, courageous charity workers with their thankless struggle. But I did have my camera, and I knew a few people working on magazines who could, just maybe, give me a leg up to that rooftop.

Then I needed brains for my plan. Not my brains, but better, bigger, well-known ones with a gift for language. And sure enough, they responded. Writers gave themselves up and added sparkle to the dust—each one nervous but each one determined to do it, all of us becoming witnesses, ready to tell what was actually happening.

Things were elemental. I knew it was cold in Armenia when the piss in our toilet froze, and I knew it was hot in Chad when the donkey next to me dropped dead like a cartoon cutout. I knew I was frightened when I wanted my mum, and I knew I was doing the right thing when I overheard a girl on a bus in London crying as she described one of our stories in *The Sunday Times Magazine*. I learned that war was pointless, and bad water killed nearly everyone, and if that didn't get you the mosquitoes did. I learned things about myself I could never have understood without the hardship and death I witnessed, or the instances of human fortitude and kindness I observed. This is where hope comes in.

I'll never forget the nurse who gave us her last cold Fanta in the most godforsaken place I have ever been, or holding hands with a woman in Sierra Leone as she gave birth, or the eleven-year-old boy with AIDS who told me to look after myself, or the thunderstorm in Sudan that raged over the grave of a baby as he was buried.

What I cannot remember is everyone who was saved, because there were too many. If ever I doubted anything, I never doubted that every time I made a cup of tea in my safe home, someone in an MSF T-shirt would step forward, through the shit, past the bad food, past the bodies and the bugs, through the unbearable heat and the total lack of thanks, and save someone's life. They did that in front of me time and time and time again, and that's really what I wanted to let you know. This book is their witness.

— *Tom Craig*

Armenia

Paradise Lost

DBC PIERRE

I'M IN A SUNNY HOUSE with an unexploded rocket-propelled grenade embedded in its cellar floor. Granted, I've had some brandy. I look out onto the back garden where white mountains rise, humps of ice cream towering into a cobalt sky. The lesser reaches of the mighty Caucasus; just there, in the garden, sparkling, where the bird table should be. And I struggle to reconcile the extremes of this place.

Noah's Ark came to rest in Armenia. Leopards still roam here. Apricots and cherries originated here, as did wheat. All still rustle wild. Armenian minds disproportionately dot the catalogue of human achievement. Forests whisper with oak and almond, pistachio and wild jasmine. The first Christian state arose here. Winston Churchill declared the brandy finer than any cognac. And it remains impossible to pass a dwelling without being invited in for coffee and chocolate, if not brandy.

Paradise.

I'm in paradise with a live missile. It blasted a hole through two solid stories and, without even exploding, set fire to the roof. It's one of eleven lobbed over the mountain one winter's day. The others went off. With typical hospitality, the man who owns the house takes me down to see it. It's there, stuck two and a half feet into the floor, at a slight angle. Waiting. Outside in the sun it's supposedly minus twenty degrees. In here it feels minus thirty. The man mutters, frowns at the projectile, and kicks it.

There's a pause. We remain unexploded.

Leaving the house for the warmth of an icy, still sunlight, I take in the mountains around us, and, even having breakfasted on brandy, immediately pinpoint the man's problem: a hostile border straddles them. Azerbaijan, a bullet's flight away. We stand for a moment, gazing. A man dressed like a shepherd passes on the road behind us, somehow absorbed into himself. I raise a hand. Then I turn back to ask the obvious question: how does the man with the missile live with such a threat in his house? He tells me he's moved his family of six into the garden shed, until the missile is made safe.

"And how long have you lived in the shed?" I ask.

He crinkles his eyes, has an empty chew behind his whiskers. "Thirteen years," he eventually says.

I look up toward the border.

"But I have many acquaintances in Azerbaijan," adds the man. "I'll ask them to come and fix the thing." He looks at me, a smile creases his face. "Come—we'll have some brandy."

Nothing prepares you for Armenia. My stated aim was to get as close as I could to the Caucasus without getting shot; but the journey I'm about to embark on is wilder than fiction. For all her ripe beauty, her whimsical charm, I see hardships here that challenge belief.

I've come to sniff out Transcaucasian settings for the heroine in my next novel, *Ludmila's Broken English*. At least that's what I thought when I boarded the plane. But my stupid duty-free bag, my pointless choice of chicken or beef for dinner, the asinine tinkling crap on the plane's speakers, all became an insult to reality when we finally ploughed the mists over Yerevan and set down on a runway carved into snow and ice. Within memory of those little comforts—the little plankton-cloud of ego-floaters that is our Western sustenance—I sat in a stench of shit and piss for lack of running water in the one-room apartment of an eighty-three-year-old woman. She said to me: "When the war started, I wanted to bring my family to safety. It was midsummer. My son, my daughter-in-law, and my grandchildren—an eight-year-old, a six-year-old, and a six-month-old baby. I made them go in a different car to me. But the Azeris set them on fire. I went to the hospital to find them. But there were five coffins there, made for them."

With the unraveling of the Soviet Union, Armenia—Hayastan as she's known here—was the first firework in the Transcaucasian chain to go off. Now watch the rest of them bang. She has an unfriendly border with Turkey to the west, the result of Turkey's refusal to admit the genocide of one-and-a-half million Armenians early last century. She has an actively hostile border with Azerbaijan to the east, after the bitter conflict that raged from the late eighties into the early nineties over the disputed Armenian enclave of Nagorno Karabagh. The only open route left is north to south, from Georgia to Iran. And with war came a wholesale repatriation of Armenians and Azeris into their respective territories, whole villages being swapped in some cases, furniture, livestock, and all. For most, however, it was an ugly flight. Luckier families were merely forced from their homes in the clothes they stood up in; intermarried couples and their children were split apart.

But not too many steps away from the old lady wearing socks over her boots for traction on the ice in her apartment, I begin to learn that war isn't the whole story here. The story of this small, landlocked jewel between the Black Sea and the Caspian is more deeply layered still.

The man with the missile comes to best symbolize Armenia's situation for me. Malicious fortune blasted into her house over a decade ago: the earthquake of 1988 that took more than 20,000 lives and made 500,000 homeless; the eruption of hostilities with her larger neighbor, Azerbaijan; and the collapse of the Soviet Union, under whose control she enjoyed a measure of stability and growth. At the time there was much attention paid to her plight, and helpful forces rallied from near and far. But as the flashpoint passed, as more exotic and pressing catastrophes caught the popular mind, much of that support melted away. And as high-priority crises grew out of control here, important strands of more basic existence fell into neglect.

More than a decade after the announcement of ceasefire, much of Armenia still lives in a state of poverty, her infrastructure in decay. Pensions, when they're paid, amount to little over six pounds a month, yet fuel costs approach those in America. A young republic for the third time in her history, Armenia has no mineral resources to speak of and relies heavily on Diaspora Armenians for support.

And as I stand here, she still struggles to find the tools to clear the mess the 1980s lobbed into her house. In a world intent on the immediacy of conflict, on the savage, career-making, newsworthy glamour of unfolding crises, this forgotten place seems a bitter taste of things to come.

The taste of a chronic and festering aftermath.

With occasional shelling and sniper fire still erupting around the eastern defenses, and having been told in one town that the mayor has a new gun and might be out shooting stray dogs on the street, I hook up with a team from Médecins Sans Frontières, who have large "No Kalashnikov" symbols plastered over their vehicles. These suddenly seem more helpful than the skull design on my snowboarding jacket.

It turns out MSF came here in the immediate aftermath of the 1988 earthquake and just never left. When issues of front-line care were dealt with, MSF crews saw a disturbing residue emerge from the depths of the culture. As a result, and unusually in the world of front-line support, the medical charity decided to channel some of its resources into a project that deals with perhaps the most vulnerable target of trauma and neglect: mental health. From a regional base in the lakeside town of Sevan—a collection of glum Soviet buildings scattered over a high plateau, with a decrepit ferris wheel strangely creaking in the wind at its entrance—young Belgian psychologist Dr. Luk Van Baelen leads me on a journey into the dark world of the uncared-for mind.

Nothing could have prepared me for what I was about to see.

Not far from the house with the missile sits the border town of Chambarak, comfortably settled into the folds of a high valley. The town is a mixture of rural rusticity and post-Soviet neglect, an occasional apartment block rising between traditional houses of lava and stone, and smatterings of hay and dung. Some windowsills sport old US Aid tins as flowerpots or buckets, souvenirs of support long gone. A nutty haze of dung smoke hangs over Chambarak, from ubiquitous solid fuel heaters like large iron shoeboxes with stovepipes attached. The town's market building is a vacant shell, attended every day by a crowd of heavily wrapped men doing nothing and talking about doing nothing. Only one trader is there, selling twigs for broomsticks.

"There used to be nearly 100 percent employment here," says a man. "Now it's nearly 100 percent unemployment. Every day there are five funerals, but never a birth."

The man, like half the town's population of around six thousand, is an Armenian refugee from the town of Artsvashen, seventeen miles over the mountain in Azerbaijan. He left everything behind to flee the war. With the border so close, combat fatigues and military fur hats are more in evidence on the streets here. Armed watchtowers look down from the mountains. When we take our jeep off-road to view the town from a hillside, soldiers quickly appear out of the snows and make toward us. We vacate the hill.

Wandering the icy streets of Chambarak—little more than compacted humps of ice glacially layered with hay and dung—I come to note that there's a feeling around a place that has had shells lobbed at it. Bombs sensitize, not de-sensitize, as is often romantically supposed. There's a quivering nerve that stays raw and bleeding long after the gunfire has stopped.

In the middle of the town there's an old Soviet block that was once either a prison or a collection of miniscule apartments without plumbing. It stands gutted and derelict. Van Baelen takes me inside. "When I first saw this place," he says, "I knew immediately why I was in Armenia."

A fetid stench upholsters the block, sharpening as we move upstairs. The building has been stripped to bare, sooty concrete, and in places genuinely gutted by fire. Litter migrates in icy drafts. Some flights up, noises can be heard behind a door. We knock. The door opens onto a cloud of dung smoke from a wood stove, thick enough to burn the eyes and throat. In one room, just big enough for a single bed, a small table, and a dresser, sits a woman called Hamest. Three children sit with her. They are refugees. They fled Azerbaijan fifteen years ago. The building is a refugee hostel. A handful of families are camped there still, waiting for a change in their fortunes.

And there's something more: a curiousness, an unexpectedness in the makeup of the family's features and in their manner. The boy has a strangely elongated face and a detached, doleful gaze. Then the father arrives and bids us welcome. And there's something unusual about him too, behind his beard and in his eyes.

Hamest and her husband are mentally retarded. So are all their children. And their life's routine after the door closes behind us is one of unthinkable abuse. Hamest's husband often trades their bread for vodka and drinks with other men in the building, often in that tiny room. He regularly beats Hamest, and there is reason to suspect her daughters suffer sexual abuse at the hands of the men. Hamest's mother is dead, and she has lost all contact with the family she knew when she fled Baku, Azerbaijan's capital, in 1990. She is utterly powerless.

MSF provides Hamest with a grant for electricity, and its psychologist tries to convince her to send her adolescent daughter to a boarding facility, away from the horrors of home. But Hamest is afraid she will lose her daughter as well. I retire from the building with questions. Not least, what are the odds of a mentally handicapped couple finding each other, and going on to raise a handicapped family?

To discuss and absorb what I've seen, we make for a river gully just outside town. Here, two old portable cabins and a gazebo-like garden shed sit wide apart from each other in the snow. One of them is green and houses a kitchen. The other sheds hold a table each with chairs. Between them they form a restaurant. Barbecued pork and traditional flatbread are served, with pickled, seaweed-like greens and luminous green pop tasting of melted Strepsils. A woman trudges forty yards each way across the snow, back and forth with our food. The tiny gazebo ends up having comfortable seating for eight. We dub it the Pork Tardis.

I learn that Hamest's problems don't end with the men at the refugee hostel. When her husband is out, ranking soldiers from the local base come to the hostel for sex. The kindlier officers might sometimes leave a bag of pasta or a loaf of bread for her troubles. The hostel's inhuman feel palls over me. As it is, I'm staying in an old Soviet apartment in Chambarak, without running water, and with only intermittent power. The snow around its entrance has compacted into gray ice, and a puddle of bright blood, hopefully from a freshly killed animal, gilds its shine. Suddenly it is relative luxury.

On another edge of town, we visit a rustic house whose yard is absorbed by a tower of hay. Animals orbit noisily. A young, bearded man in an old sports jacket tends the stack with a pitchfork, and waves. Inside the house I meet Anoush, a pretty, young woman with quick eyes and a bright, earnest demeanor. She is a refugee who has found a way out of the hostel. She speaks in crisp Russian.

"On the 13th of January, 1990," she says, "nine people came early in the morning to our apartment in Baku, when we were asleep. They came in and slammed the door. I had three very young children. The men asked to see our passports. When they saw our Armenian surname, they told us to get out."

Without even putting on her socks, Anoush went to the police. They sent her to gather with other Armenians in a cinema, before loading all onto a bus for the border. She had a different family then; her husband was an Azeri seaman, away in the Caspian for a fortnight at a time. He was away that morning and never knew how or when his family left. They haven't seen or spoken to him since.

After years in the refugee hostel, and with small children to care for, Anoush was literally facing starvation. Her escape came when she was married off to a retarded deaf mute—the man outside—by his parents, who wanted him taken care of. He brutally beats her. Her children suffer nightmares and are being counseled by local MSF staff, but she is finding it difficult to keep up her own visits to the psychologist and social worker. Her husband's parents—whose haystack, livestock, and stove she lives with—are against it.

A more successful escape has been made by a woman I meet named Tamar. She once lived near the man with the missile in his cellar and also had the experience of a rocket-propelled grenade crashing into her house. Except hers detonated on the dining table. She watched her mother-in-law explode. It kicked off a living nightmare, forcing Tamar into the hospital with psychosis. She later spent ten years at the refugee hostel in Chambarak, with neither heating nor a window in her room. But MSF staff have since reunited her with her own mother and stabilized her condition with counseling and medication. They provide ongoing support to help keep her out of the institution.

Emerging from these visits into sparkling sunlight, into the natural gloss of the place, is bizarre. Snow twinkles like tinsel here, swirling off ridges and rooftops in gusts as dry as dust. We travel the snows to a town called Drakhtik, whose population of around fifteen hundred is made up entirely of refugees.

No less than half are mentally disabled.

Translated, the name of the town means: "Little Paradise."

I'm invited to take coffee and chocolate with the mayor of Little Paradise, himself a refugee. He takes me to a dilapidated office with a wood-burning stove, an abacus, and an old typewriter in attendance. His assistant is a nurse in a laboratory coat, who fusses with the coffee on the stove. When we begin to discuss the war, she chips in with lurid sound bites. "One woman watched her sister doused in petrol and set on fire!" she chirps. "Even people in the middle of a wedding party were thrown out of Artsvashen!"

The mayor tells me Drakhtik was once an Azeri town, similar to the Armenian enclave at Artsvashen, where he came from. With the outbreak of war he was instrumental in forming a council to swap properties with the Azeris who lived in Drakhtik. The entire town was swapped for Artsvashen, and both sets of townspeople given two days to relocate.

But this was a civilized elite. Within Drakhtik there is also a refugee hostel populated by the many who missed out on a swap.

I learn that both Hamest and Anoush, the women married to abusive retarded men, first stayed at the hostel in Little Paradise. Then I learn they are sisters. The odds can't be calculated. Moreover, I hear of a third sister, Vardouhi. She became severely psychotic after their flight from Baku and is in a psychiatric hospital. She hasn't been heard from in eighteen months.

We travel around Lake Sevan, the beautiful blue hole in the doughnut of Armenia, toward the town of Vardenis. There sits the psychiatric hospital where the third sister is to be transferred. Between potholes in the road, and mindful that there is no legally enforced side of the road to drive on, I grapple with the apparently widespread phenomenon of mental disability here. More than one Armenian has told me it stems from the Azeri habit of intermarriage within immediate family. But, understandably, this isn't the only thing I've heard blamed on Azeris by Armenians, and, in fairness, I haven't met an Azeri to counter the claim—nor am I likely to, as I'm told Azerbaijan won't admit visitors with Armenian stamps in their passports.

What is probably true, after some investigation, is that traditional cultures on both sides of the border believe marriage is good for the mentally disabled, even thinking of it as a kind of remedy, a stabilizer. So disabled offspring are married off and abandoned to family life, where they conceive more disabled children.

We travel long, stark stretches, breathtaking stretches of snow and mountain and high plateau. At one point a man on the road flags down the MSF jeep to ask if we will dispense him some Tramadol. We come to another border town where a new MSF primary healthcare clinic sits reeking of paint. A vivid crowd of female health workers gathers inside in overcoats, high heels, and lashings of makeup. A sort of Mean Machine of care. But there are no patients. It must be minus twenty degrees in the building. Vapor billows from our mouths. The sight of an examination table with steel gynecological stirrups brings a wince.

"The power's off," explains the chief doctor, tightening her coats. We all look through the window onto the Southern Caucasus, as if power will somehow return from there.

This clinic is all the district has in the way of free basic care. Apart from Armenia's vestigial Soviet framework, which doesn't much encourage visits to the doctor, the World Bank has, with characteristic wisdom, instructed the government to develop a private, user-pay system for healthcare. Except nobody has the money to pay.

Care at the psychiatric hospital, however, is free. But you don't have much say once you get there. Making our way to the hospital,

I brace myself for dark realities. We're met by the hospital's director, a softly spoken man with the bearing of a Russian golf pro. In his office, a table is laid with brandy and chocolate. It's ten o'clock in the morning. He plays us a video of the hospital's last Christmas party, opened to the community in an attempt to soften perceptions of mental disability. The hospital's chief doctor joins us, a dentist by profession.

A brandy, a toast. We turn from the television to chat. As the bottle empties, the video party scenes end and more salacious programing plays beneath, featuring dominatrixes in lingerie and boots, and sensual, pumping music. "Be sure and call me for the next Christmas party," I tell the director. He turns to the screen. Laughs. Another brandy, another toast.

Conditions are not unpleasant as we tour the largely rebuilt, freshly painted buildings. Even without brandy this would be true. MSF invested heavily in the facility over the course of a decade, handing a greatly improved hospital back to local authorities. A party rages in one common room, with Armenian clarinet and drum music squealing from a portable machine. Still, I'm approached twice in the corridors by patients begging for help. One smartly dressed man folds a carefully written letter into my hand, imploring me to help with his release. For a moment I'm prepared to believe there are sinister oppressions afoot behind closed doors, such is the man's apparent normality, indeed, erudition. Then he says he has high-level contacts in the FBI. They are waiting to help him on the outside. The chief doctor shakes his head, we move on.

The second patient to approach is a middle-aged woman who speaks to me in fine English. She is a doctor of electronic engineering, an author of various books and manuals, and a psychotic. I must say here that the tension of contrasts on the journey is kept alive by our interpreter, Tatevik Avetisyan, a young woman so fluent in Armenian, Russian, and English that there is literally no overhang between what she hears and says. And when the English-speaking patient begs me for help to escape, tells me she's cured, and the chief doctor gives Tatevik a warning to pass on to me—without blinking, Tatevik explains that we should move along lest we cause unease, and she does so in fluent Spanish so as not to upset the woman.

We visit a common room for more profoundly disturbed patients. Some sit lifeless and frozen, others writhe improbably. All seem in a good state of physical health, the atmosphere is light, the room's space is sunny. Dr. Van Baelen spots one deeply psychotic patient frozen over a chessboard. He initiates a game with the man. The man quietly beats him in ten minutes flat. The game turns into a series. Van Baelen eventually wins.

As the tour proceeds, the pleas of the English-speaking patient sit heavily in my mind. Looking around, it becomes clear that some of these patients would be at large, leading normal lives, if they were in Europe. Many of their disorders are easily controlled with medication. Yet they remain here, often for years, or for life. I ask the director how this can be.

"When a patient comes here," he says, "we're duty-bound to take all the details we can from their next of kin: their address, their telephone numbers. But I'll tell you this: if I went to the files and phoned every patient's number today, visited every address, more than half of them wouldn't exist. The families have moved on, they've changed the number, didn't give the correct address in the first place. They can't be found. So there are patients here who could be out, but because there's nobody to sign for them, nobody to see they take their medications, they can't be released. That's the problem we face."

Sixty percent of the patients here will never leave. The hospital has its own graveyard.

MSF has become instrumental in the hunt for relatives of those committed to institutions like this, as well as in a patient's release and reintegration with family. In one house I even sat at the table of a lady—an indomitable matriarch, whose strict enforcement of my participation in the feast she'd laid out with brandy pretty much wrote off the rest of the day—who, with MSF support, has taken a patient into her home who is not a relative. With such meetings a picture began to emerge of the net MSF is building around the wider problem here, by providing early counseling and psychological support to prevent conditions developing, by assisting confined patients who could be cared for in the home, and by trying to break down cultural barriers that lead to stigma and neglect.

But it remains an up-mountain battle.

Next day in nearby Martuni, I meet the region's chief psychiatrist. He occupies an office in a seemingly deserted polyclinic that stands alone in the snow like a disused railway station, winds howling through its open concrete foyer. It's bitterly cold inside. No power here either, and the building seems largely empty, only debris and litter visible through darkened doorways. A nurse ushers us into the psychiatrist's office. When Dr. Mikayel Kahramanyan arrives, he goes to a cabinet at the back of the room and produces plates of freshly sliced fruit, nuts, chocolate, soft drinks. And brandy. It's ten thirty in the morning.

"You have to have a drink," he shrugs, "it's just too cold." A delicately patterned tablecloth appears, covers his desk, and the refreshments are laid out. The doctor sits without removing his jacket or his Russian-style fur hat. He bears a passing resemblance to Anthony Hopkins.

He agrees there are many institutionalized patients who could be released. But he says the country is still dealing with old Soviet structures, and even older cultural attitudes. In Armenia, a psychiatrist's report is needed to obtain many types of certificate and licence, including a driver's licence. Many people just won't put themselves forward for treatment, as a psychiatric file would blight them for life. So their conditions are left to worsen. Families shun members with psychoses, and if sufferers aren't committed by their families, they eventually come to the attention of police.

"The problem then," says the doctor, "is that nobody will claim them back into the family home, where they can be supervised. If they're released on their own recognizance, they feel cured and forget, or neglect, to take their medication. They suffer an acute episode, they're brought back in, and so the cycle goes."

I ask the doctor if things have changed much since Soviet times. He nods, and pours another brandy. "Of course they have," he says, raising his glass. "The biggest change is that I can sit here and talk about this with you."

I met a great many people in the Southern Caucasus. And it may be, notwithstanding psychoses brought about by the trauma of war and dislocation, that there are no more mental disabilities here than anywhere else. But there's a great stigma placed on mental disability here, and it attaches to anyone within reach of a sufferer. Sufferers are alone with their problems. Lesser conditions like depression and anxiety are ignored altogether, just taken as another fact of hard life. And this dynamic forms the heart of Van Baelen's project. He has made a start on the task of destigmatization.

Chambarak opened its first MSF day center in 2003. There is one in each of the towns I've visited, staffed with psychologists, social workers, and assistants. They are a hub not just for the disabled, but for the wider community; if only for warmth, coffee, and conversation. Every weekday the center is open for counseling, crafts, music, fitness, anything that brings the twain together in a relaxed and constructive way. Picnics and open days are mounted whenever possible. The able and disabled are mingling.

"We use any excuse for a party," says Chambarak's psychologist, Loussine Mkrttchian. Subscription is steadily growing at her center.

It's also at the day center I see a remembered face. The shepherd who wandered past the house containing the missile. I meet him. His name is Petros, a handsome, weather-beaten, profoundly retarded thirty-five-year-old with airs of great musing and reflection and a fixation with the buttons on his coat. A familiar sight around the district, he simply wanders from morning to night, often in the mountains, often around the prohibited border zone.

His family feeds him, but that's as far as his care goes. He's been left all his life to wander. He has never spoken a word.

Within a year of the center opening its door in Chambarak, Petros was lured in off the mountain. Now he's here every day, for as long as the door is open. He seems to feature in every snapshot in the center's bulging album. On weekends, when the center is shut, Petros can be seen sitting on the doorstep. Waiting.

And in the days since I was there, he's also started to speak. His first words were, "Good, good."

Luk Van Baelen's captaincy of this MSF project will soon end. Local MSF staff have been trained to take it over. And like the little lifespan of a dog within his longer life here, my journey has ended too. Van Baelen stands in the bright cold, watching beneficiaries' horseplay on the steps of Chambarak's day center. I ask him if he's looking forward to returning to Europe. He says he doesn't plan to return. He hasn't been back since the project began.

"I just know if I went back," he says, "the first thing I'd hear is someone complaining that their train was five minutes late." He squints out over the snow, up onto the mountains. "I just don't know if I could handle it."

We walked into a clinic in what felt like the middle of nowhere in rural Armenia. The electricity was not working, as usual. As a result, the doctor and her team of nurses were working in sub-zero temperatures wearing their winter overcoats in this pristine MSF clinic. This kind of resilience and determination to keep going is a benchmark of the organization.

Below: The light on Lake Sevan.   *Right:* Mother and son.

Left top: One of the many refugees in the local area bids farewell to his child as he goes off to work for the day.

Left bottom: Lunch in one of various cabins dubbed "The Pork Tardis," where we were fueled with local pork and brandy.

Below: The place where a rabbit was killed.

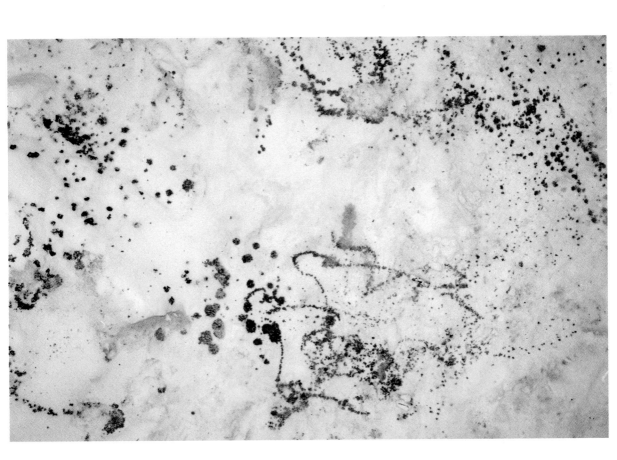

We were welcomed everywhere we went in Armenia with a toast of local brandy. Regardless of the time of day, our hosts made it very difficult to say no. On this occasion we were treated to a generous dose or two by the chief of the local hospital who then walked us to the secure wing of the psychiatric ward. This particular moment was fraught with a heady mixture of morning drunkenness, frozen noses, and deep apprehension as to what lay behind the door ahead.

Below: In the middle sits Hamest surrounded by her children—all refugees from Azerbaijan. She has suffered years of systematic abuse from both her husband and the local soldiers.

Right: This is Petros (whom DBC Pierre called the Handsome), a weather-beaten wandering shepherd who had airs of great musing and reflection as well as a fixation with the buttons on his coat.

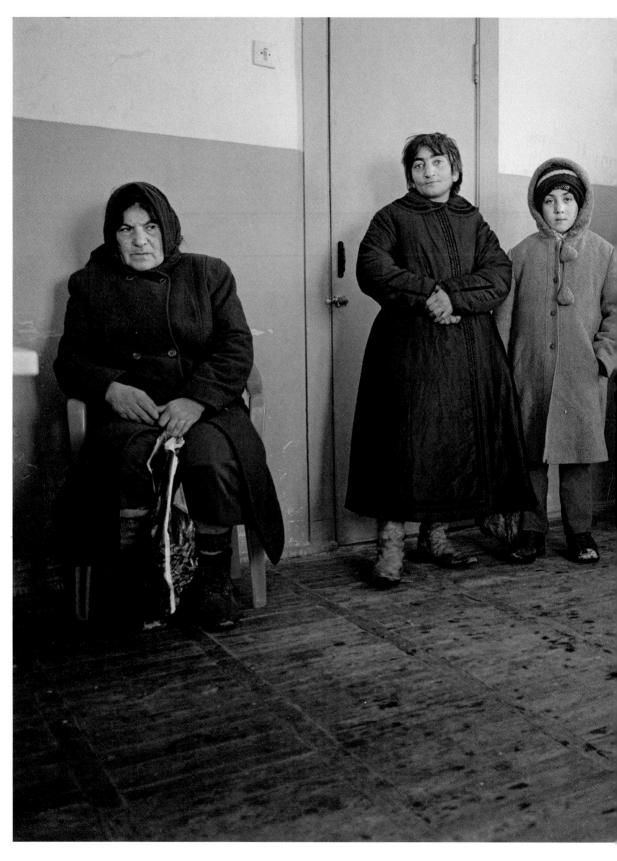

Each day scores of people turn up at the clinic for hot soup and bread—among the few antidotes to the biting cold.

Assam

The Nowhere Clans

HARI KUNZRU

A CARPET OF VIVID GREEN paddy fields stretches away toward a range of hills. Though the monsoon has just begun here in Kokrajhar district, cyclists and brightly painted trucks have to pick their way over a pitted road, which will only deteriorate as the rains set in. We bounce along a stretch of causeway past lines of villagers stooping to pick rice or set nets for tiny fish and frogs. The scene is attractive, as long as you don't think too hard about the backbreaking work, or the flimsiness of the huts clustered by the roadside. It could be anywhere in rural India. It certainly doesn't look like a war zone.

Yet Kokrajhar is a place where, depending on who you talk to, somewhere between 100,000 and 300,000 people have been driven from their homes by years of communal violence, where government officials work with armed guards at their office doors, businessmen live in fear of kidnapping and extortion, and a fragile peace is barely maintained by a massive Indian army presence.

The district is part of Assam, the largest of India's northeastern states, an area wedged between Myanmar, Bangladesh, and Bhutan that has spawned an alphabet soup of militant groups, all with their own grievances, political agendas, and thirst for funds and recruits: the AAASS, ACMF, ANCF, ASF, and the ATF (that's just the A's), the Hindu Liberation Army and the Muslim Liberation Army, the Muslim Liberation Front, the Liberation Tigers, the United Liberation Militia, the United Liberation Front, and so on. Nearly forty organizations are thought to be active, some representing the interests of a particular ethnic or religious community, others aspiring to carve out their own new "united" nation in this particular corner of India.

The troubles of "The Northeast" (a phrase that takes in Assam and neighboring states like Manipur and Nagaland, which have their own insurgencies) are little known outside India. The obscure politics and the protracted, low-intensity nature of the various conflicts don't grab international headlines in the style of an acute humanitarian emergency. This probably suits the Indian government, which prefers to concentrate global attention on its economic boom, or the glamour of its film industry. Unlike Kashmir, where local religious and communal tensions have taken on geopolitical significance, Assam's woes are still an internal affair.

Not being news doesn't make life any easier for Joseph Tudu, the headman of Sapkata camp. Tudu is a slight, wiry, black-skinned man, with the self-effacing shyness of someone who is used to hard work and ill treatment. He also happens to be a Christian priest. One night in May 1998, his neighbors started breaking down doors in his village and slaughtering the people inside. He took his family and fled to the nearest safe place, which happened to be the local police post. The Tudus set up camp outside, hoping that the presence of the policemen would be enough to protect them. Incredible as it seems, they were joined by several thousand others who had just been through the same terrifying experience. Six years later they are still there.

Sapkata is a kind of limbo, an embryonic village that, like other long-term camps around the world, exists only because there is nowhere else for its inhabitants to go. The people of Sapkata did not run far—only a few miles in some cases—but their old lives might as well be on another planet. They are too scared to return to their homes (if those homes still exist). Their former neighbors farm their old fields. Joseph and the others supplement their government rice ration with day labor, sometimes for the very people who drove them out.

Joseph takes me on a tour of the camp, through a maze of low, mud-walled huts. Men loll on wooden bedsteads, children playing at their feet. Women peer around doorways. They have the impersonal curiosity common to very poor people around the world. When a rich man goes past, you stare, but only in the way that you might stare down a well, or out at the horizon. There is something self-protecting in this blankness. Allowing yourself to be fully conscious of such a stranger's humanity would be unbearable. After all, this is a person just like you, no better. Yet with his 2,000 calories a day, his dental and optical care, his access to antibiotics, and above all his height, his very physicality testifies to the existence of a world of such opulence that it makes a mockery of your own. Better this cosmological distance. Better to imagine him as a cloud, a bird, a ghost.

So a certain wary attention follows us past the pumps where the people draw water and over to the stinking open latrine where they deposit their waste. There is a hopeless and slovenly feel to these parts of the camp, at odds with the huts and their neatly swept floors, their walls decorated with relief designs of flowers or Christian crosses. There is a reason for this contrast. Indian government policy aims to "rehabilitate" the people of Sapkata. There is a program to encourage them to leave the camp and set up homes elsewhere. The carrot in this situation is a resettlement payment. One of the sticks is the official ban on digging a well or installing proper sanitation. A decent infrastructure would give this place greater permanence, which the state doesn't want. So Joseph and his people suffer all the grim and degrading consequences of dirty water: diarrhea, parasites, cholera, and, above all, malaria.

When the rain comes down (as it does over me on the second morning I spend in Sapkata) the baked earth instantly dissolves, and you find yourself up to your ankles in thick, brown mud. The light changes and the muggy heat goes out of the air. When the rain recedes, it leaves behind a world of standing water, of paddies and puddles and lakes and ponds and ruts—a paradise for the malaria parasite. The dominant variant found here is plasmodium falciparum, which the medical textbooks dryly describe as "the most pathogenic" of the four species. If P. falciparum finds its way to the brain it is capable of killing its host. In Sapkata, where the government hospital is half a day's walk away, it frequently does.

The only foreigners in Kokrajhar are my own hosts, a medical team from Médecins Sans Frontières who are running clinics in four camps providing basic health care and malaria treatment. At Sapkata they have converted a disused government building into a waiting shelter complete with bamboo benches onto which up to four hundred people cram three days a week waiting to see Dr. Anup and Dr. Swapan, two young Indian doctors. Marshaling the crowds is Jeri Merritt, an American nurse striding around in scrubs. She towers above the villagers, the kind of woman you'd expect to play a pioneer in a fifties Western, wearing a gingham dress and carrying a shotgun. The pace is relentless. Patients are weighed and their temperatures taken. Too high? They get a paracetamol to bring it down. The worst cases lie on the ground at the front, attended by family members. Everyone is tested for malaria. The first morning I attend the clinic, more than half the patients are positive.

Frederick Hembron is typical. He is six years old and fell sick three days ago, but he likes school and insisted on going until he was too weak to continue. When the doctor tells Frederick's mother that her son has malaria, I expect her to look shocked or anxious. Instead she just nods. I find her reaction inexplicable, cold even, until it dawns on me that for the Hembron family, malaria is just one of those things; it's not an exotic tropical disease but an everyday ailment. Every rainy season a lot of children have fever. Sometimes they die. That's just how it is.

Resignation and humility. Another day, at a clinic in Runikata camp, I watch a woman carefully wet the soles of her feet in a puddle before stepping onto the scales to be weighed. The gesture is both humbling and somehow upsetting, the sign of someone who feels privileged to receive even this basic level of care. I see many such things in the camps. Here are people who are used to being last in line, who have internalized the world's idea of them as the lowest of the low.

It's not just the residents of the camps who use the MSF clinics. The organization has a policy of treating anyone who comes to them, so side by side on the bamboo benches sit all the people of

Kokrajhar, local villagers as well as the people they displaced. The villagers are Bodos, a tribe that is thought to have migrated here in the distant past from somewhere farther to the east. They look Burmese or Tibetan and speak their own Sino-Tibetan language. The women waiting with their babies at the clinic are dressed in horizontally tied saris woven with bold patterns of brightly colored stripes. They look very different from the women of the camp, who are slight and dark and wear plain saris, one end thrown over the shoulder. The Bodos consider this part of Assam their rightful home and refer to it as Bodoland. The landscape is dotted with stelae decorated with Bodo shields and swords, commemorating the "glorious martyrs" of the struggle for independence.

On a wall by the roadside: One Homeland, No rest! Tomorrow we'll win victory! Nearby: Your money, your state, your property, your life. Crush Militants!

Unfortunately for those who dream of Bodoland, Assam is tea country. Growing, harvesting, and drying tea is a labor-intensive process, and in late imperial days, British plantation owners needed more workers than they could find among the Bodo. The solution was to import laborers from Bihar and West Bengal. This last sentence doesn't give a sense of the immensity (and the arrogance) of the project, which was a full-scale piece of social engineering. Whole tribes of forest dwellers, who had always lived on the margins of Indian society, were uprooted and taken to Assam. These "adivasi" (indigenous or aboriginal) people were considered in traditional Hinduism to be "ati-sudra"—lower than the lowest untouchable castes. To the British, the Santhals, the Mundas, the Oraons, and the other groups they transported to the tea gardens were "criminal tribes," who had frequently rebelled against them and needed to be controlled. Since the 1840s the Adivasis had been gradually displaced from their forests, a process that independence has done nothing to abate, carried on now in the name of wildlife preservation or development. To the British, the tribals were landless and disorderly. Transporting large numbers of them to pick tea solved two problems at a stroke.

What happened after the British departed is explained to me by Dr. Ashish Bhutani, the deputy commissioner of Kokrajhar. Outside his office a detachment of armed policemen lounge around on plastic chairs, clutching their rifles. Inside, Dr. Bhutani, a career civil servant who was posted here three years ago, seems dwarfed by the problems he faces, or perhaps just by the enormous desk behind which he is sitting. The desk is truly a monster, inlaid with tiles and arrayed with every imaginable kind of blotter, phone, penholder, and lamp. It is faced by a triple row of red plush chairs.

Clearly Dr. Bhutani is used to receiving deputations fifteen or twenty strong. Though there is a line of junior functionaries waiting to see him, the DC has read about my last novel in the *Times* of India and is keen to talk. The functionaries will have to wait for their papers to be signed.

We have a souvenir photo taken. The desk yields up a pointer, and Dr. Bhutani pulls a cord on the wall. In a dramatic gesture a curtain sweeps open to reveal a large-scale map of the district. I half-expect to be given a sealed envelope of orders. "Everything you see above here is forest," he tells me, drawing an imaginary east-west line somewhere below the camps at Sapkata and Runikata. I am confused. I remember the area as open farmland. When I mention this, he smiles wanly. It is clear I have fallen into a trap. "Exactly! It is forest, but only on paper." Dr. Bhutani then unfolds a story of law and the effect of legal abstractions on human lives.

It seems that in the last twenty years, illegal logging and land clearances have completely changed Kokrajhar. Once the district was covered with Sal trees. This useful hardwood was exported all over India for use as railway sleepers. When the government last surveyed the area, a quarter of a century ago, it was natural to categorize it as forest. When a forest becomes a bureaucratic forest, there are certain consequences. A forest has no farms or villages, let alone camps brimming with Internally Displaced Persons. Therefore there is no need to provide infrastructure or medical care. A person who lives in a forest (unless they are lucky enough to be a resident of a "recognized forest village") is not supposed to be there. A community in such a place does not exist.

Yet above Dr. Bhutani's line, not existing, is a poor, mixed, and growing population. Pleas from Kokrajhar officials for their masters to recognize the de facto nature of the change have always met with the curt rejoinder that they ought to view things ecologically. Official government of India policy is reforestation. More forest is the answer. "Derecognizing" this existing forest would set the nation back, greenwise.

During the last twenty years the Adivasis, used to sustaining themselves partly on the dwindling resources of actual nonabstract areas of woodland, have found themselves in unaccustomed conflict with the Bodos for land, food, and jobs. The two communities coexisted more or less peaceably until the 1990s. Then, as Bodo nationalist sentiment was fanned by the increasing stresses and strains of shared life, armed militias were formed. The situation was made worse by a new wave of largely Muslim migrants, escaping hard times in Bihar and West Bengal. In 1995 the first wave of organized violence was directed against these newcomers. Thousands were forced to flee. In 1996 the Bodo militias, growing in confidence, conducted the first of several massive pogroms against their old Adivasi neighbors, which left more than a thousand of them dead.

It's easy to get hold of small arms in this part of India. Just to the east lies the lawless and heroin-rich golden triangle. There are porous borders and neighboring states that don't mind at all if the Indian government has a few extra problems on its hands. Soon Muslims and Adivasis had formed their own militias and embarked on a program of ugly retaliatory violence. Stories collected by human rights groups make grim reading. A Bodo woman pulled off a bus and beheaded. Twenty Muslim loggers hacked to death with machetes. A grenade thrown into an audience of Adivasis as they watched a traveling movie show. The security forces, given extensive powers to "keep the peace," initiated their own wave of terror. Political activists disappeared. Young men were beaten to death in police stations, and village women were raped by patrols. The army, present in ever-larger numbers, was said be operating a "shoot to kill" policy when conducting raids.

In December 2003 the Bodos were granted limited local autonomy in the form of a "Bodo Territorial Council," and several of the main militant groups signed a ceasefire. In the last few months businessmen and village headmen have still been kidnapped in Kokrajhar; people have still been found dead by the roadside; army patrols occasionally come under fire, but larger-scale incidents have died down. Dr. Bhutani is plainly not optimistic that this state of relative calm will persist. Digging deep for positivity, he turns the conversation to the local government's "civil action program," banging on about tree planting and gifts of handlooms to tribal women. In the middle of this he mentions that the district runs a camp where surrendered militants are being "rehabilitated," fitting them for return to ordinary civilian life. I ask if I can visit. To my surprise he picks up the phone.

So begins an unsettling afternoon. From behind his monster desk Dr. Bhutani calls the police superintendent with jurisdiction over the camp. A couple of hours later I find myself in front of a smaller desk in a stifling office, as a trio of policemen brazenly discuss (in Bodo) their tactics for handling my problematic request. These senior officers give off an unpleasant vibe. Maybe it's just their ghoulish, red, paan-stained mouths. Maybe it's the unhurried way they are handling this, the little power plays they use to emphasize their authority. They are the sort of men who enjoy inspiring a little touch of fear now and again. I wonder what it would be like to be an Adivasi youth in their custody.

Eventually, one of the three is directed to take us (myself, Tom the photographer, and two MSF staff members) to the camp. What I have in mind is a short interview, perhaps with one or two former militants and a translator, in which they explain to my tape recorder why they took up arms, and why they laid them down again. A few quotes for this piece. Straightforward.

Sarah, the MSF project coordinator, is visibly nervous. She is British, a veteran of several missions who speaks in a clipped and somehow geographically dislocated accent, the result, perhaps, of many years of communicating with people whose first language is not English. When I first meet her I ask if she is from the Western Isles of Scotland. She looks baffled and tells me she grew up in the Midlands.

When Sarah doesn't like the way a conversation is progressing she smiles and nods. In the police superintendant's office she is doing a lot of it. She trained as a nurse and, like many of the MSF volunteers I meet in Assam, seems instinctively to prefer to look at Kokrajhar from a medical rather than a political angle. In a way it is this gut medical perspective that makes MSF work. Their aim is to provide care for people who desperately need it. The business of who did what to whom and why, who is the victim and who is the aggressor, from a doctor's point of view, is an irrelevancy. To this extent, medicine cuts through the Gordian knot of politics. However, being a representative of a foreign NGO in a volatile area like Kokrajhar is inevitably a highly politicized role, never more so than when negotiating a relationship with local government and security forces.

At home in Britain we watch the crisis on TV, the crisis that is always going on somewhere and is always framed in the same way, with the same shots of nursing mothers and drought-struck farmland and thin, young men in army fatigues waving rifles. When the reporter kneels down and lets a handful of dry soil run through his fingers it means famine. When he puts on his blue body armor and crouches in front of a ruined building, it means civil war. We watch this familiar story and think, they should do something about this. Why don't they just go in and sort it out? We rarely stop to unpick what "going in" entails, the delicate negotiations, the many shades of compromise. The politics of aid, whether it comes as food or development or medical assistance, necessarily preoccupies organizations like MSF, who have to be on their guard against any appearance of complicity or cooptation. A mistake could lose the trust of a local population, or upset some group whose compliance is necessary for the logistics of a mission. So the most important principle for an international NGO working in a place like Kokrajhar is neutrality. Getting too close to the police or army, and particularly being seen in the company of security forces, is something MSF teams try to avoid: for example, traveling in convoy with a police jeep on the way to some kind of detention center. No wonder Sarah looks troubled.

So the MSF driver deliberately dawdles on the road, letting the other vehicle go on ahead and putting visible physical and ideological distance between the agency and the police. Once we arrive at the camp and see what awaits us, that distance becomes harder to maintain. Before today MSF had no idea this place even existed. Believe the police and it is some kind of cross between the Priory and a job center, and even to a skeptical eye it doesn't look like a prison. There are no guards, no perimeter. Instead a collection of housing blocks is arranged around an open maidan. Some opportunist has set up a paan stall outside. Men, women, and children stand and watch us arrive.

We are led into a long meeting hall, and I realize this interview is not going to be straightforward at all. Fifty young men are sitting cross-legged on the floor, facing a line of plastic chairs. When we enter they get up, adopting the "stand easy" pose of soldiers in drill formation. Despite their civilian clothes it is clear they are used to military discipline. Immediately the police inspector starts to address them in Bodo. Accompanying him are two young men who are introduced as representatives of a local NGO. They are to act as translators, yet as the inspector barks out his speech they are worryingly vague about what he is saying. "He is introducing you," they tell me. It sounds more like a set of orders. What is happening? Have these men been coerced into attending this meeting? Are they being warned not to say certain things, or instructed to behave in a certain way? As they are lectured they look at the floor with studied neutrality. I catch the eyes of my companions. None of us is comfortable.

One of the NGO workers stands up and makes another introduction, in which I catch my name, and the phrase "Medicine San Francisco." Sarah is beside herself. "Sans Frontières," she calls out, in her precise voice. "No Borders. We are a neutral organization."

"Medicine San Francisco," though funny, is not good. Post 9/11 and the war on Iraq, being associated with America or American foreign policy can have dire consequences. In Afghanistan the mistaken identification of the organization with a U.S. agenda has led to attacks on its staff. Repeatedly we interrupt to ask for more translation. None is forthcoming.

Then it is my turn. I am expected to introduce myself and ask my questions to the group as a whole, like a lecturer with a class. It is undoubtedly the weirdest public speaking experience

41

of my life. The heat is oppressive. Some kind of large spider is climbing up the back of Tom's chair. I say I am a writer and would like to know why they took up arms. Some of the men nod and murmur. What purports to be a translation of this question lasts a suspiciously long time, and then there is a long pause, until someone sitting near the back gives what may or may not be an order, and a man farther forward stands up and starts to talk in a rapid monotone, as if repeating a chunk of poetry rote-learned for school. These "surrendered militants" are evidently still subject to some kind of discipline from senior cadres.

The young man's speech goes on for a long time. Only fragments make it into English. He is an ex-member of the National Democratic Front of Bodoland and is passionately listing the names of ancient Bodo kings and heroes, using their illustrious memory to confirm his people's historic right to the land. It does not sound like the speech of someone who has lost his convictions, let alone been "rehabilitated." I ask how old he was when he began to fight. He was fourteen. He is now twenty-one.

For form's sake I ask a couple more questions, though all I can think of is how to draw the whole farce to a close. I feel I have been complicit in something but have no way of knowing what. The police inspector claims these men will soon receive a large sum of money and travel to the state capital to receive, of all things, business and new media training. I look at the sullen faces of these Web designers of tomorrow and wonder if this is true. Afterward one of the "NGO workers" takes me outside and tells me that in his opinion, the former militants are only here because they were separated from their leaders during a recent antiterrorist operation in Bhutan. "The reason they have surrendered isn't because government has offered them one lakh or five lakh rupees. Their leaders isolated them and the common people didn't support them. That is the only reason." He shows me an ID card, so I can check the spelling of his name. It was issued by the Assam Police Force. The "nongovernmental" bit of being an NGO is obviously loosely interpreted in Kokrajhar.

We let the police leave first, then drive away. I try to work out what just happened, what has come from this untranslated entanglement of writer, photographer, aid agency, and security forces. It piles in on top of many images and conversations, the jumble of the last few days: Renuka, the MSF health educator at Sapkata, who lost several of her family members in the pogroms and hopes to do postgraduate work at Gauhati University; the chirping of millions of tiny frogs in the rain; Mr. Panjikar, the modernizing manager of the local tea estate, striding through his bushes with an armed guard, to protect him from kidnap;

Mr. Panjikar's swagger and bravado—"I'll not pay! Let them come!";
the table listing compensation rates for animals killed on the road
(50 rupees for a chicken, 3,000 for a cow); the young army officer
who served us tea and pakoras, assuring us that his posting was
"a picnic" while outside his sikh soldiers stripped and cleaned
mortars and heavy machine guns. A swirl of impressions of a place
that is, on a global scale, only ordinarily unhappy. Against the
confusion and moral compromise of the camp for surrendered
militants I can oppose the memory of another afternoon's walk,
following a German doctor called Kirsten Resch through a camp
at Deosri, close to the Bhutanese border. She was looking for a baby
girl whose case had worried her on a previous visit. She found the
baby unattended in a dark hut. Her prolapsed anus had become
infected, a livid red bulb hanging below her filthy smock. It was
an image of squalor and physical abjection, yet there was no hint
of disgust as Kirsten examined the child, only tenderness and
compassion. A cliché, no doubt, this image of the doctor and the
little brown baby, the stuff of aid agency ad campaigns. But in the
gray area of Kokrajhar it seemed to stand for something, a moment
of focus, a brush of the fingers from an ordinarily inattentive world.

The monsoon in Assam washes away the roads and provides the mosquitoes with much-needed breeding grounds, making life doubly hard in the ongoing battle with the voracious malaria problem.

At every MSF clinic,
the registrar must bring
administrative order to
the countless patients.

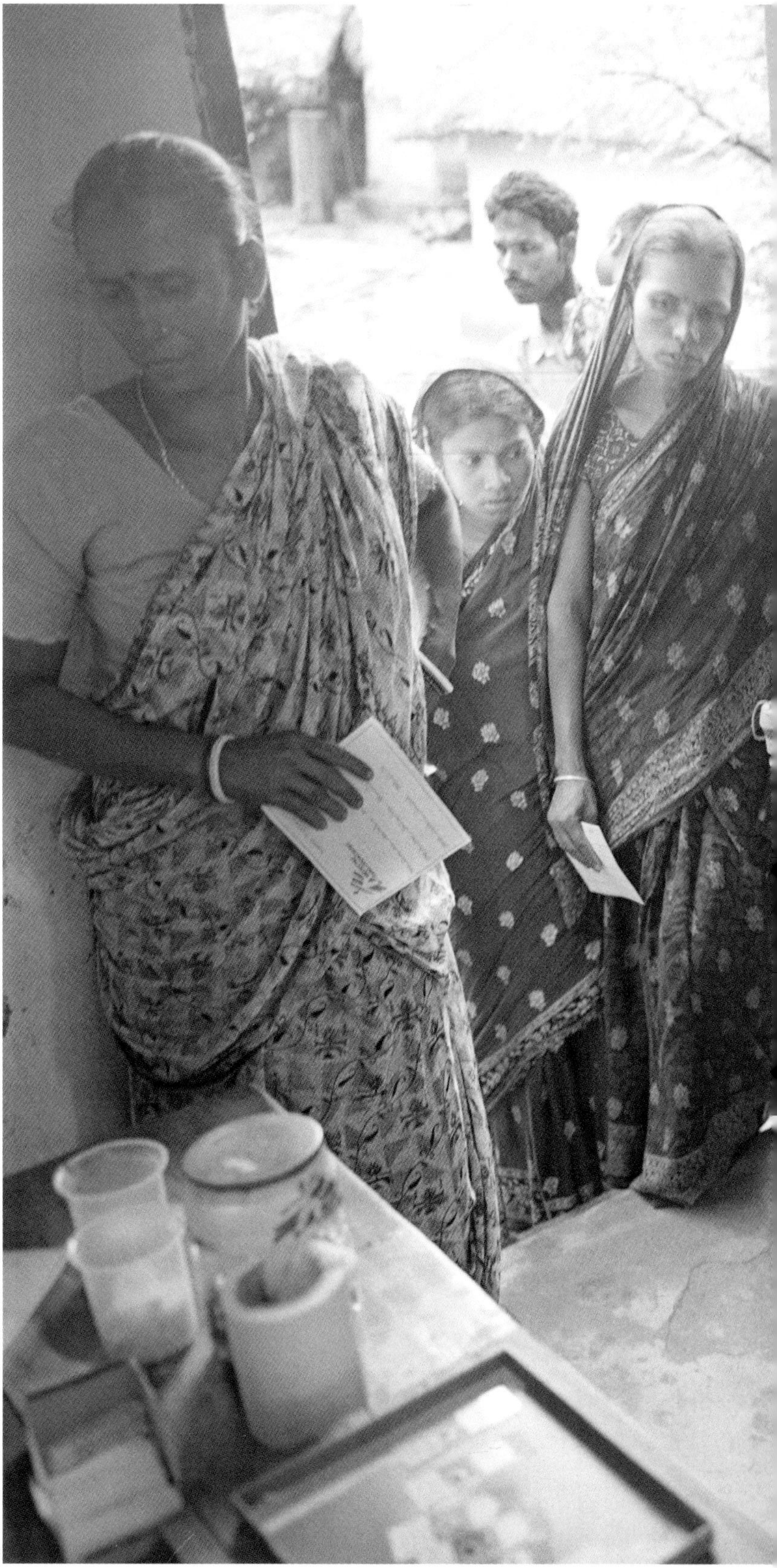

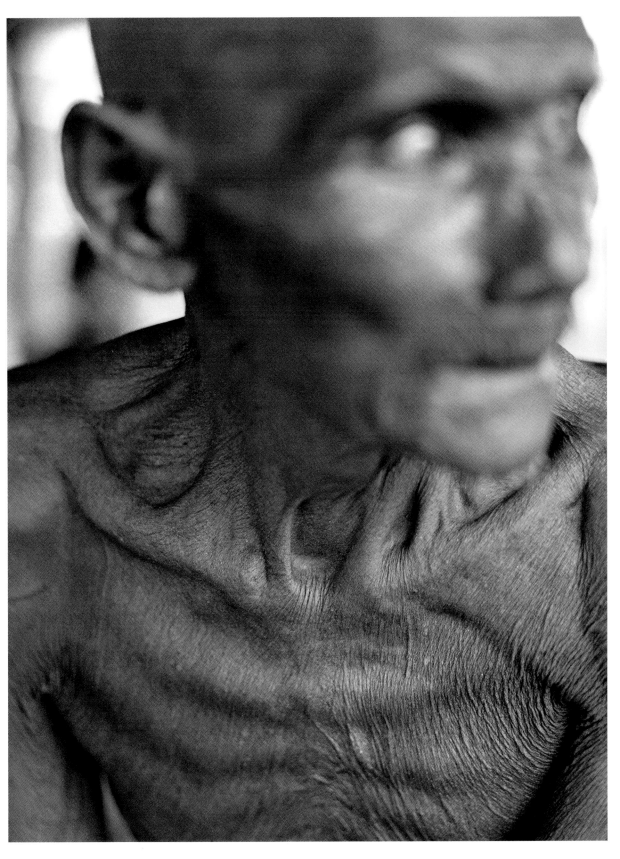

These were the medical implements from the clinic prior to the arrival of MSF—another poignant reminder of the progress MSF is making.

Previous spread: Illness manifests itself in many different physical guises, depending on the strength of the individual. This man was unforgettable. It was as if he was made of mahogany. His skin was stretched like a drum over his skeleton beneath.

A portrait of a grandmother and granddaughter: one was so frail and the other so shy. It was incredibly touching how utterly involved and responsible the young girl was in trying to help her grandmother get better. In developing countries, children become responsible for their elders many years before their European counterparts.

Burundi

In Another Life

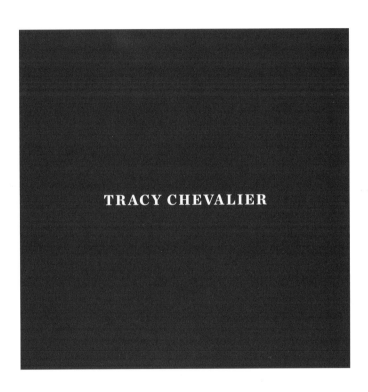

TRACY CHEVALIER

THE ANONYMOUS BROWN METAL GATE we approach is not far from the city market and the bus station in the center of Bujumbura, the capital of Burundi. At the sound of our car, a guard opens a slit at eye level in the gate, looks at us, then slowly opens up. We drive into a large garden where a one-story pale yellow house sits. The grounds are enclosed by a high wall and consist mostly of scrubby grass and high weeds that a man is cutting with a scythe; clumps of bougainvillea, palm, and banana trees provide needed shade.

Women and children are clustered on the steps of the house. As we come close they stare at us, and I try not to stare at them. We step inside. It is cool and calm here in the waiting room. More women and children are sitting along the sofas and chairs. Women have been arriving since 6 a.m., some of them walking in or taking buses from the countryside. Some are accompanied by family or friends. Others—like a local schoolgirl in her blue and white uniform, or a sixty-year-old grandmother of sixteen from the north—chose to come alone. More are coming in all the time; by the end of the morning the room will be overflowing. It is Monday morning. It has been a busy weekend for some. Most of these women and girls have been raped.

I came expecting to see tears and grimaces, hear shrieks and cries, but the women are impassive. They speak quietly to their companions, or to strangers they meet in the room, but mostly they sit silently, waiting. Children wander in and out. A five-year-old girl raped four months ago sits on the floor in the sunlight playing with wooden dolls.

Partly the subdued atmosphere may be shock—some women, like the schoolgirl, were raped just hours ago. Partly it may be a desire to quell emotions in front of strangers. But the lack of drama may also have something to do with the Burundian character itself. Again and again I am told that, unlike in other African countries, people here don't show much emotion; everything is hidden. It's true that while I am in Burundi I don't see people laughing or shouting quite so much as in other places I've been. Except for the children—they smile and laugh and run after me just as much as children elsewhere. Something must happen to Burundians at adulthood—unofficially considered to be age twelve, when many stop school and some even marry (though the legal age for marriage is eighteen)—that makes them push feelings under the surface. Perhaps that is why rape flourishes here more than in many countries: it is easy to hide it when everything else is hidden too.

Bujumbura sits on Lake Tanganyika; across the lake hangs a wall of forbidding mountains like something out of *Lord of the Rings*, with the Democratic Republic of Congo beyond. The Congo is by all accounts a mess, and airs its problems publicly;

rumors proliferate about savage killings, systematic rape, even cannibalism. By comparison, Burundi seems sedate. Bujumbura itself is a straightforward African city, with decently paved roads, constant electricity, a huge market, banks, shops, schools, even a public swimming pool. For all its apparent orderliness, however, Bujumbura is rife with violence and lawlessness; its middle-class neighborhoods are walled off with guards for each house. There was a civil war in Burundi between 1993 and 2002, and although it didn't succumb to the large-scale massacres its neighbor Rwanda has become infamous for, it shares similar ethnic tensions between Hutus and Tutsis, as well as an erosion of the social fabric that normally reins in illegal activities and antisocial behavior. The postwar Burundian government is still an interim one, awaiting the elections that will turn it into a real democracy. Although the war tore it apart economically and socially—it was ranked 173rd out of 177 countries in the UN's 2004 Human Development Report—nonetheless Burundi feels like a country with a chance, on the verge of improving enormously. However, Bujumbura is ringed with foothills hiding guerrillas opposed to the government. The city is under curfew, and there is gunfire at night.

The Women's Health Centre we are visiting was opened in September 2003 by Médecins Sans Frontières. It offers medical treatment and psychological counseling for people who have been raped. Previously such victims had gone to MSF's long-established Centre for War Wounded in another neighborhood. There women and children coming in who had been raped might well find themselves alongside their rapists, being treated for gunshot wounds or fractures. It became clear that women needed a place where they could go and feel both protected and anonymous. Besides taking in rape victims, the Women's Health Centre also offers family planning and treatment of sexually transmitted disease (STD), partly as a cover so that people won't assume that everyone coming in has been raped. Rape is its primary concern, however. It now receives 150 rape cases a month, whereas only five to ten per month come for advice on family planning.

Most victims of rape come initially to get antiretrovirals, medicine that can prevent HIV infection. It needs to be administered within seventy-two hours to be effective and has to be taken for twenty-eight days. There has been a widespread, effective campaign to educate the Burundian population about AIDS, and people here are terrified of it, though in relative terms it is not as bad a problem here as in other African countries: 8.3 percent of adults are HIV-positive in Burundi, compared to 20 percent in South Africa, 25 percent in Zimbabwe, and 36 percent in Botswana. Most rape victims come to the MSF clinic initially to obtain the drug, but are also medically examined, tested for STD, and counseled by a psychologist. There are follow-up appointments one and six months later.

The clinic is run by women, with only the guards, the drivers, and the gardeners men. The place has a calm, purposeful, practical energy about it. In fact, I notice that about women in general in Burundi: though they wield little economic or political power, they remain the dynamo behind the wheels of society. Women here never sit idly by the roadside the way men do. They are always doing something: carrying water, selling things in the market, tending children, working in the fields with baby strapped to back. Even their clothes are more vibrant—they wear colorful sarongs and head scarves, while the men tend toward western T-shirts and trousers.

The local staff at the center are well educated, well trained, and well dressed, and manage that tricky balance between the sympathetic and the practical so needed in situations like this. I am not so deft. When I try to talk to women who have been raped I hesitate to ask for the details of what happened to them. I feel tripped up by the myriad emotions the idea of rape brings with it, wherever it occurs: horror, embarrassment, prudishness, voyeurism. At one point I sit out on the steps with an older woman and another schoolgirl, both of whom speak French as well as Kirundi, the local language. They are both here for their six-month checkups. I ask them lots of questions that skirt around the main topic but bottle out of mentioning rape directly. It feels too stark and disrespectful to say, "So, about your rape—tell me what happened."

Célestine, one of the psychologists at the center, is not so squeamish. She shows me an outline of the questions she runs through and issues she covers with each victim. They range from specific details of the rape—Where did he touch you? What did he say? Did he hurt you? Did you cry?—to questions about other aspects of the victim's life that have been affected. How do you feel about your body? Are you able to sleep? Do you worry about safety? Who do you feel you can talk to? By talking them through what happened, she helps them to purge themselves of the experience. Célestine may well be the only person they feel they can talk to.

I sit in on a session she conducts with Françoise, the sixty-year-old grandmother, and a widow of several years. She wears a green, yellow, and orange head scarf, from which black and gray curls poke out. Célestine makes constant eye contact and half-smiles as she speaks softly and calmly with Françoise, keeping her talking. Though I don't understand Kirundi, it sounds like Françoise is telling her what happened in great detail. She shows little obvious emotion, except that now and then she leans to one side and puts a hand to her forehead. "She's ashamed that a woman her age would be raped," Célestine explains. "She hasn't told anyone and never will." She's only come to the clinic now—two months after the rape—because she's got pain in her abdomen. (Tests reveal Françoise has contracted an STD.) She lied to her children about why she's come all the way to Bujumbura.

At the end of the session, Françoise looks directly at me for the first time. "I want to know about you," she says. That seems fair, so I tell her what I can and show her a photo of my son. "Only one child?" she says. "I thank God that I have had so many children!" I take her pity on the chin. When I promise to keep her secret safe, Françoise smiles at me. I have changed her name for this piece, as for all of the rape victims and their families.

Françoise's age is relatively unusual. The majority of rape victims in Burundi are under eighteen, and many are very young girls—perhaps because they are clearly virgins and thus will not pass on the AIDS virus. A few rapists even believe that sex with a virgin will cure them of their own HIV status. I hear of other superstitions as well: sex with a dwarf will bring you luck; sex with an old woman will bring you wisdom.

At the center I meet girls five, ten, fourteen, and seventeen years old who have been raped. The youngest victim I meet at her home, about ten kilometers from Buhiga, a northern town where MSF recently set up another sexual violence center, alongside a hospital it supports and a nutrition center. Christine is two years, ten months old and the previous week was raped by a houseboy. The atmosphere here is lighter than you would expect, given what has happened. In part this may be due to decent material circumstances. The house—a hut by western standards—is bigger and better built than others I sat in, made of new local bricks and a tin roof, and another building is under construction. The kitchen floor may be packed dirt, but it is full of food—branches of bananas, tins of oil, sacks of manioc flour. There are two beds and a table with solid wooden chairs rather than stools made of boxes. Christine and her mother, Beatrice, wear clean, new-ish clothes— Christine in a white dress and striped sweater, Beatrice in a red and white shirt, a green and white sarong, and a scarf hiding her hair. Beatrice has five boys and another girl, all in school as we talk. An eleven-year-old neighbor looks after Christine when Beatrice is working in the fields or selling lenga-lenga—a leafy vegetable similar to spinach—at the market. Clearly they are better off than some if she can afford to send so many children to school and pay a houseboy too. Here even the poor hire others poorer than they to help out.

Money helps, of course, but the atmosphere I attribute largely to Christine and Beatrice themselves. Christine is a solid, feisty little character, and the moment I meet her I know she's going to be OK. Most children her age who have been through such a traumatic experience would be terrified of strangers, but Christine is only momentarily put off. Soon she is giving us good long looks, her round face curious, her chin set, her gaze straight. She obediently stands with her mother for a photo taken from the back but can't resist looking around at Tom—not peeking timidly, but staring, sizing him up.

Beatrice is equally charismatic. A small woman with a fine-boned, expressive face, she speaks in a soft voice that still carries, like a well-trained singer. She is clear in her beliefs, and it is easy to see where her daughter gets her determination. Mother and daughter are obviously crazy about each other. As we sit inside while a sudden rainstorm hammers on the roof, they keep their arms wrapped around each other, Christine happy and cheeky on her mother's lap.

Christine was left alone with the houseboy—actually a man of eighteen—for only a short while, but sadly it was long enough. Beatrice had gone to the fields, the other children were at school, and the babysitter went out for a moment to get some milk. When she returned she found the man on top of Christine. He ran off but was caught and is now in jail. Christine showed her mother what happened with the houseboy using gestures. Beatrice took her to a nearby doctor, who confirmed that she had been raped, though it appears that she was not completely penetrated—which may be good news for her future, as virginity is highly prized and a necessity if a girl wants to marry.

Christine has not cried since just after the rape, nor spoken of it. But at night she has nightmares, and her mother holds her close then as she does now. "I love her so much," Beatrice says. Eventually I find out that Christine is likely to be her last child—Beatrice is forty-four—and that three other daughters have died. Children are so important to women here that usually the first question I ask them is how many they have. They tell me how many boys and girls, but there is always a ghostly third number lurking behind the others—the number of children who died, of the usual killers: cholera, malaria, typhoid, malnutrition.

All seems well now with Christine and her mother, except for one factor. It is easy to forget the fathers in situations like this. Beatrice's husband is a soldier and lives in a camp that the rest of the family moved from a year ago because they had found it hard to make ends meet there. They came to where they were able to buy a piece of land, but it means that the father has to live apart from his wife and children. Christine's father knows about the rape now—Beatrice sent a member of the family to tell him. She thinks he will come back to them in two days, on Saturday. According to her, it is for her husband to decide what should be done about the jailed houseboy. She is Christian and believes in forgiveness. "When my husband comes back," she says, "if the man accepts that's he's done something bad and asks for his forgiveness, my husband will give it because he knows God. It is not for us to judge him."

Whether Beatrice's husband will be so forgiving toward her is less certain. She fears he will be angry, perhaps at his daughter but more likely at Beatrice. Beatrice's face tightens. What can she do to placate him? Allison, the MSF coordinator, offers to speak to him about the medication Christine is taking and to explain that it isn't Christine or Beatrice's fault. But all of us women in the room—mother and daughter, MSF staff and me—know that it is difficult to stem the tide of a husband's fury at his wife. Throughout Saturday I wonder if he has arrived home yet, if he has hit Beatrice or Christine or thrown them out. I wonder still.

Léocadie is one of many women at the Bujumbura health center remarkably open about speaking of their experiences and willing to be photographed head-on, even when given many opportunities to say no or be photographed from the back or in silhouette to preserve anonymity. The center is careful to make the records of these women confidential, using an elaborate code system and locking records away. The stigma of rape is very strong in Burundi—as it is in most places. Rape victims are not named in newspaper reports in Britain either.

Léocadie is twenty and lives in a distant province; she took a bus to get to Bujumbura. She has a one-month-old son wrapped in blue and yellow cloth, whom she breastfeeds while we talk. Her son keeps his eyes fixed on her as he feeds; when he opens his mouth to yawn, his tongue is white with milk.

She was raped when she was almost five months' pregnant. She sells maize in the market; sometimes when she doesn't have enough from her own field, neighbors give her some of theirs to sell. One day a neighbor offered her some of his, leading her to an isolated corner of his field and then raping her. "He was very strong," she says. "He put a hand around my throat and the other over my mouth." He did not seem to care that she was visibly pregnant.

Léocadie is here for her six-month checkup and has found out that she is not HIV-positive. That is one stroke of luck in her life. She was not so lucky after her first visit to the clinic: she remained for a week so that her pregnancy could be monitored, and when she returned to her village she discovered her husband had left her because of the rape, taking their three-year-old daughter with him.

Léocadie has seen her daughter just twice since then and says she and her husband are "divorced," though possibly not in the legal sense. She has also moved from the village, after neighbors were mean to her, and now lives among Christian neighbors who she says are much kinder. She used to run into her attacker's wife and would say hello but little more. They never discussed what happened. The man has run off; that violent moment in the cornfield has broken up two marriages.

Throughout the interviews, I ask women why the men did it. They give concrete answers: Satan made him; he was badly brought up; his father also raped women and he inherited the urge; he is a madman; he wanted a wife. None said anything about how badly women fare generally in Burundi, or the male domination that keeps them so downtrodden. They are fatalistic, which may explain why Christianity is so popular here, with its promise of a better life after death. None of the women's answers really gets to the heart of the question: why do men do this to women? This is not a question limited to Burundi or third-world countries. Men rape two-year-old girls in Britain too, and no one knows why. Though I may be disgusted and upset by what I hear from Burundian women, it is not the response of the righteous, but rather the wary nod of recognition.

At least in Britain rapists are punished when caught. In Burundi all too often they go free, even when they are known. One boy, whose thirteen-year-old deaf and mute sister was raped by a neighbor, told me he still sees the man in the market sometimes but will do nothing because the man's family has threatened his if they try to go to court. In several other cases the man is in jail but is unlikely to be tried—delays and costs often put victims' families off. MSF refers victims who wish to pursue justice to organizations such as Avocats Sans Frontières (Lawyers Without Borders) that try to help. ASF has seen just two cases from the MSF center through to a court ruling (one found guilty, one acquitted) and is now working on forty more rape cases referred from various organizations.

That doesn't mean the victims have given up on justice, however. "I want him to die in prison now," declares Alice, a spirited ten-year-old who was raped the previous day by a neighbor's son while her mother was at Mass (60 percent of the population is Catholic). Her mother, elegant in a purple satin dress and head scarf, looks a little embarrassed at her daughter's headstrong response. "Perhaps he should just remain in prison forever," the mother modifies. Actually, I think to myself, Alice got it about right.

On our last day we visit Josephine, just south of Bujumbura in a neighborhood made up of people displaced by the civil war. Such neighborhoods are chronically poor and lack the social cohesion of a more established community. It is full of people who have lost everything—home, job, family—and radiates vulnerability. The director of the local health center tells me they receive on average eight rape cases a month—though there are surely many more committed—and the rapists are often government soldiers or members of former guerrilla groups that have been absorbed into the army and prey on those least able to fight back.

Josephine is sixteen and has a one-month-old son whose father is her rapist. She has a catlike face, with high, wide cheekbones, slanted brown eyes, and full lips drawn around a small mouth. She wears a yellow shirt and a blue and green sarong, and sits with me on a woven mat on the dirt floor of an empty room. Josephine shares this and another room (also empty except for a plastic mat she lays her son on) with a widow who has taken her in. I have begun to understand what poor means in this country, and this is as bad as it gets—no furniture, no food, no clothes but what she has on.

Josephine used to live out in the countryside with her parents. They were killed in 2002, toward the end of the war. She has no brothers or sisters. She ended up in an area for displaced people in Bujumbura called Kiname, where ten months ago unknown robbers broke in and raped her. Neighbors heard her cries and helped her get to a local health center. She was passed between various local associations—of which there are surprisingly many—which ended up moving her to this new neighborhood. Josephine's upper lip wrinkles with almost genteel scorn when asked about her circumstances. "I would rather be back in Kiname," she says. "It's not so poor as here."

She has few opinions about the direction her life has taken, why she was raped, or what will become of her. My questions slide off her and begin to seem ridiculous. Cushioned by material well being, health care, and education, I have the luxury of ranging far away from the present—analyzing the past, anticipating the future. Josephine, however, lives completely in the moment: she does not dwell on her wretched past and shrugs when asked about the future. I have never met anyone so completely disconnected from the continuum of time. Past and future may as well not exist; there is only her son's open mouth that needs filling, his body to be washed and clothed. She asks for food—she admits she doesn't eat every day, even though she is breastfeeding—for clothing, for soap. Those are her immediate needs.

Josephine is the last woman I interview before I leave Burundi, and she abruptly enlarges the picture I have been focusing on all week by refusing to engage with the trauma of her rape. I ask her at last which has affected her life more, the rape or the war. "The war, of course," she responds promptly, "for it is still affecting me." She gestures at the nothingness around her. She is polite with her answer but I feel naïve to have asked such a question. The rape at least gave her a son, the one concrete, positive thing in her life. "He is my future," she says, much more concerned about him than any possible future husband.

When Tom suggests that she cover her face with her hands to preserve her anonymity for the photos, Josephine thinks for a moment, then reaches up and pulls the polka-dotted scarf from her hair and winds it around her face, leaving one eye exposed. It is a confident gesture worthy of a fashion shoot; in another life, with her bee-stung lips and her self-possession, Josephine might have been a model. In another life, she might have been many things. She is here, though, and her hand-to-mouth existence is likely to be punctuated by hunger, hardship, and loss until she at last loses her own life. She stands in the doorway holding her baby and watching us go, and I feel I have lost her already.

The first of many women I photographed at the medical clinic for rape victims.

Léocadie was raped when she was five months' pregnant. When her husband found out, he left, taking their three-year-old daughter with him.

Below left: Beatrice and her daughter Christine, who was raped before her third birthday.

Below right: Sixteen-year-old Josephine lost her parents in the war. She was raped by robbers who broke into her place at night. She has a one-year-old son whose father is the unknown rapist.

Almost every woman and girl we met had been subject to frightful ordeals at the hands of men. I constantly questioned whether or not I should have been photographing this story at all; as a young man, I felt my presence was an imposition. This innocent little face in the crowd seemed to say something about how we were both feeling about each other's presence.

This little girl was only five when she was raped. These little wooden figures are used as a tool to help children describe their ordeals. It was as if nothing was untainted.

This man came to the clinic
for victims of rape to collect
his eleven-year-old daughter.
I couldn't begin to comprehend
the anger and confusion they
must have felt.

Cambodia

The Paradox of Progress

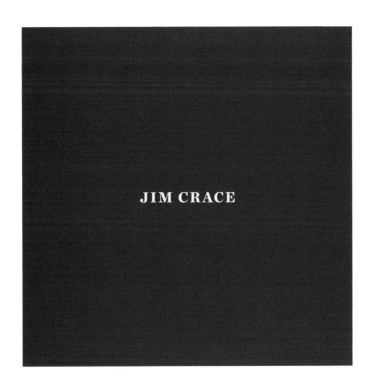

JIM CRACE

THE VOLUNTEER FARMERS who bare their skin throughout the night and offer their blood to the mosquitoes of Pailin are taking grave risks for a good reason. Armed with a flashlight, some cotton wool, and a test tube each, and with their trouser legs rolled up, they wait until an insect, attracted mostly by the carbon dioxide in perspiration or breath, alights on their skin to feed, and then to capture it for the laboratories of Phnom Penh, where its disease-bearing parasite levels can be assessed. In this remotest district of Cambodia, tight up against the Thai border on the northern slopes of the Cardamom Mountains where the Khmer Rouge fought its final battles, the tropical mosquitoes are among the world's most deadly. A single unlucky bite and any one of these eight human baits, working in four-hour shifts, could be infected with Japanese encephalitis. In the past six months almost a thousand southeast Asians have died from it, and many thousands more are facing paralysis or brain damage. Or these volunteers could become the bone-aching, hemorrhaging victims of dengue, which is at its most virulent during this season of monsoons and which, though not normally lethal except for children and the very old, is incurable. According to Richard Veerman, my MSF host, who has himself only just recovered from the fever, "You can do nothing about it but sit out the pain and hope not to die."

But it is neither dengue nor encephalitis that should worry me most when I sit down on the boggy ground with my back against the hemp hedge in the tiny, rain-soaked village of Pang Rolim to join the volunteers and bare my own leg to the mosquitoes. Nor is it the deadly Russell's vipers or the cobras that are common in the soybean fields just yards behind us. Nor is it even the undetected and undetonated landmines, which, according to a recent UNICEF report, make these farmlands "one of the most dangerous places in the world." What should have kept our legs covered is the knowledge that the anopheles mosquitoes of Pailin or, more specifically, the single cell plasmodium falciparum malaria parasites that live in them and us, were the first in the world to develop (through overprescribing and incomplete dosing) a resistance to chloroquine. This is the drug that for decades has been humankind's main defense against malaria. I have suffered from malaria before, in Sudan, and I survived with little more than a debilitating fever, but that was the less deadly P. vivax strain, which has yet to develop resistance to drugs.

Yet my fellow volunteers and I are not being foolhardy. We can be relatively confident that whatever the parasite load of the vectors filling their abdomens with our blood, we are unlikely to contribute to the worldwide toll of 2.7 million malaria deaths each year (out of the at least 350 million—almost exclusively poor—people who, according to a UN report of May 2005, become sick with the disease). In this fortunate village at least, there is a new and readily available treatment for P. falciparum, a cocktail based on artemisinin, an extract from sweet wormwood. But it has to be administered swiftly. All the locals understand from the too recent and bitter experience of neighbors that to contract this strain of malaria in Pailin and leave it to its own devices is to invite a rapid and painful death. After a week or more of gestation, we could expect fever, muscle pains, and headaches, explains Bart Janssens, MSF's medical coordinator. For any victims beyond the reach of artemisinin, however, diarrhea, nausea, and anemia might develop. And then, finally, in a third to a half of all cases, there would be "severe complications," including brain damage, multiple organ failure, and coma. "You could be dead in ten days," he warns. "It happens. And it is a horrible way to die."

Our job that night, under the cheerful scrutiny of entomologist Dr. Tho Sochantha, from the Centre for Malariology, was to help verify what the rapidly falling P. falciparum prevalence and death toll have been suggesting: that MSF's volunteer-based, rapid treatment program for malaria in these forest-edge villages, where heavy shade and high humidity offer the perfect conditions for breeding mosquitoes, is "breaking the pathways of transmission" between female insects, parasites, and humans.

My own contribution to the insect survey is only modest. I seem at first to be more attractive to ants than mosquitoes. But finally, in the pitch darkness and to the midnight plainting of cicadas, I learn to recognize the weightless, fussy probing of anopheles on my shins and I begin to fill a test tube with my captives. At the end of my shift, Dr. Sochantha holds my tally up to his magnifier and, much to the delight of a crowd that has abandoned a blaring, battery-powered television set to watch a European make a meal of himself, declares my specimens to be "from a vector that normally prefers to feed on cows." He would be happy to offer me a trapper's job at any time, though. "You are a good hunter," he says. "Their abdomens are not bloated. You have captured them before they could feed." What I do not mention is that, though my leg has not been pierced, the back of my neck is already itchy and lumpy from a dozen uninterrupted bites.

Over the next few days, in the pretty, straw-roofed, stilt villages of Treng Leu and Phnom Reang (or Tree Mountain), accessible to only the toughest off-road vehicles with the most reckless of drivers, the MSF mobile malaria team and its dignified and gentle Thai coordinator, Raden Srihawong, meet up with some of their forty trained community volunteers to "mass screen" every available inhabitant for malaria. Their simple purpose is "to reduce malaria morbidity by finding more patients." The villagers, in their mixture of traditional blouses and fake Nike or Puma T-shirts and an eclectic array of hats, are queuing in the mud at the temporary canvas-and-bamboo tents that MSF has erected for medical inspection. They are the strongest-looking buildings in the village. There is a lot of barking from the distinctively curly-tailed dogs and some crying from the children. Both seem alarmed by the presence of so many strangers and so much activity. But all the adults are delighted, and a little amazed, to have so much medical attention offered for free and on their home patch. These are some of the poorest communities in Asia. Not one has a school for its children. Not one has any electricity or sanitation. Not one has water for washing or cooking, other than that provided by the heavens. At this time of the year, the heavens have provided more than generously. A week of monsoons has turned the countryside into one great puddle. People can't go anywhere if they are not prepared to wade. But for most of the year, the land is dry and baked, and the living is hard. "There are three harvests a year in Thailand," observes Bart Janssens. "But in Cambodia there is only one, and in Pailin there is probably only a half. This is a land of grave inequalities. Most of these farmers can produce enough food for six months, but then they have to catch insects and make soup from wild plants."

They also have to deal with the presence of unexploded ordinance. Amputees are a common sight, and the red skull-and-crossbones signs warning "DANGER! MINES!!" can be encountered every twenty yards, even on the narrowest of pathways. It is said that Pailin will not be entirely cleared for a further eighty years. Chea Doeurn, whose eighteen-year-old daughter, Chek Dany, is the paid malaria "volunteer" in the virtually unreachable village of Bor Thmei, has found many mines in his soybean fields. Three of their neighbors have died. Ten have lost limbs. Their home is positioned between "Confirmed Minefields" and "Residual Minefields" in the most mined area in the world and is at the end of Route Ten, where, as late as 1999 and eight years after the official ceasefire, the final skirmishes were exchanged between government troops and the last few Khmer Rouge insurgents. It is reached on foot by a newly cleared corridor that is barely a yard wide in places. Most of their neighbors are "retired" Khmer Rouge soldiers and may well have planted many of the mines themselves.

Chea Doeurn, one of the many new immigrants who have come to these remote and risky borders because there is no shortage of smallholdings to squat and farm, recounts the story of a near neighbor who lost his right leg incrementally—ankle, knee, thigh—in three separate explosions. His daughter, Chek Dany, shudders to hear of it. "Malaria is not our most frightening problem," she says, though she herself has suffered from the disease four times in the five years since her family arrived in Pailin, probably because as an outsider she has little immunity to it. On one occasion, she was so seriously ill that she reached what she calls "a staring coma." Now, as MSF's "village face," she offers malaria advice, diagnosis, and treatment to most of the 370 inhabitants within her district. But she has yet to dare to visit some of her nearest neighbors at home because the ground between them is so chock-full of landmines. "I think a lot about the danger when I am working," says Chea Doeurn, sitting on the decking of his house-cum-shop where he sells vegetables and glasses of home-brewed rice spirit which—as I can verify—must have caused some "staring comas" of its own. "But I have to farm the fields because I am a poor man. I am more frightened of hunger than I am of the mines."

The good news is, however, that at least the killer form of malaria is retreating from their lives. The 2003 prevalence survey found 7.8 percent of these rural populations positive for P. falciparum (and showed that 5 percent of the countless millions of mosquitoes were carriers of the parasite). The "positive" figure is now down to 3.7 percent. Certainly, in the two communities of the mass screening, those few villagers reporting malaria-like symptoms on this occasion and judged symptomatic when examined physically (they have enlarged spleens, for example, or high temperatures) are few and far between. Most people are marked by ink pen on their arms with an ID number and a blue A for "asymptomatic" (clear of disease). Of this overwhelming majority, only those pregnant women needing iron tablets, or children who require deworming, or anyone with a rash, an infection, or an abrasion, are sent forward to the ever-patient Raden Srihawong for treatment. But the few who are sporting the red S of "symptomatic" proceed to another set of blood tests and parachecks. Among them is No. 191, an eleven-year-old boy named Phan Mol who suffers, like too many of his contemporaries, from malnutrition. He weighs only twenty kilograms. That's less than a healthy five-year-old. He is stoic but a little fearful when Raden examines his tiny frame and hears from his mother about the vomiting and chills that have beset her son for the past three days. But Phan Mol, like most of those marked S, is lucky. He only has the less dangerous P. vivax. Raden dispenses the chloroquine there and then.

No. 67, Uong Virakk, is less fortunate, though. As the red PF(+) mark on his forearm indicates, he has P. falciparum and is very ill. He lies on his back under yet another battery-driven television set (this time showing episodes of *The High Chaparral*). He is exhausted, nauseous, shivering, and struggling to breathe. No. 82, a three-year-old girl, is PF(+) also. So are numbers 107 (a pregnant twenty-two-year-old), 149 (a young farmer), and 26 (an elderly woman, recently widowed, who has come to the village to live with her daughter and has not been exposed to malaria before). Out of almost six hundred villagers tested, only these five—that's less than 1 percent—have been in any danger from fatal malaria. In three days' time, after their courses of artemisinin, they will be cured.

Here, for once, is evidence of a medical success story: a killer disease that has had a huge socioeconomic impact on poor communities, cheaply and simply contained by the uncomplicated expedient of "bringing diagnosis and treatment to where the problem is." Indeed, I have cause to be grateful myself to MSF and its efficient strategies. Two weeks after my exposure to the mosquitoes of Pailin and back home in Birmingham, I begin to sweat and shiver. Every muscle in my body aches. I prick my fingertip and carry out the paracheck that all the village volunteers offer to their symptomatic patients and is as simple to administer as a home pregnancy test. I show negative for P. falciparum. It's vivax again. Raden Srihawong has sent me home with all the treatments, and I expect (correctly) to be well again within a few days.

Sadly, the medical success story of MSF and plasmodium falciparum does not extend to other health issues in Pailin. This is a country ravaged by war and by one of the twentieth century's most brutal regimes. Between 1970 and 1978, two million citizens—that's one third of the population—were murdered. Cambodia has not recovered yet. Its public health provisions, nonexistent under Pol Pot and scarcely any better during the ten years of the Vietnamese occupation, are still poor. The government spends less than $3 a year on health care for each of its citizens. Infant mortality rates, according to the 1998 census, are almost one in ten. Life expectancy is only fifty-seven. Most Cambodians die from conditions that are simple and cheap to cure or contain. There are, as yet, few foreigners in Pailin district. There are certainly no tourists, except for those who come across the Thai border every night for the gambling and the "karaoke bars" (or brothels). Any other outsiders who do plan on spending any time in what has been called Cambodia's "badlands" and its "Wild West" should not expect to go away entirely unscathed. Here it is not easy to stay well.

The U.S. Department of Health advises travelers to Cambodia to protect themselves with seven vaccinations. It warns against almost thirty health hazards from avian influenza—via plague, polio, rabies, and (still) SARS—to typhoid. It recommends that visitors to rural areas should always coat themselves in insect repellent and sleep under protective nets. The guidebooks advise travelers to avoid sickness by refusing salads, peeled fruits, meat products, and anything but bottled drinks. They should evade the endemic ticks, the chiggers, and the many parasitic worms by never walking in water or in bare feet. They are, of course, exhorted not to venture from a surfaced road into the land-mined countryside, "even for the call of nature; your limbs are more important than your modesty."

But any traveler who completes the exhausting, four-hour drive from Battambang along the deeply rutted red-dirt road—with its signs imploring No Hunting, No Felling, and Use Condoms—into Pailin district, will realize at once that those cautious (and expensive) lifestyles recommended by guidebooks are impossible and unsustainable even for tourists. For locals, illness is almost unavoidable, as is medical neglect, even if they are reckless enough to enter one of the dozen or so single-story buildings in the waste- and weed-filled compound that is the disgrace of Pailin Hospital, a place of Crimean inadequacy. The director is ex–Khmer Rouge and is not medically trained. "That man learned his surgery in the bush," I am told by a Cambodian who lost several of his family members to torture but is—as are the majority of his young compatriots—keen to "close the Book of Tyranny" and "bury the past." The hospital director, like many of his seventy or so medical colleagues (of whom, reportedly, only twenty show up at work each day), was given his job as a sinecure by powerful old comrades, men like the district's current (and ex-KR) military commander, Brakk Sakhorn, who can be spotted at night at his table in the Bamboo Restaurant, a sinister satellite phone at his side, or like the provincial governor, Y Chhean, who learned his administrative skills in the forests as a Pol Pot stalwart.

Certainly, the director does not seem much interested in the sick. He manages to tour the filthy and almost empty wards without addressing or even looking at any of his patients. He seems bored, disengaged, uninquisitive. A used condom on the concrete floor goes unnoticed. So does a young woman in the last hours of her life. The one male nurse will not help her either, though only five of the twenty slatted beds in his ward are in use. She is a sex worker in the final stages of AIDS. Her skin is erupting. She is spider-thin. Only her eyes—disorientated, exhausted, and terrified—are not reduced in size. The only care she gets is a pile of damp sawdust under her bed, to soak up her feces and urine. She has been offered no medicines, though antiretroviral drugs—available in some areas of Cambodia—might have saved her life. No one is feeding her or making her final days remotely comfortable. It is not until five volunteers from Family Health International arrive at the hospital that this once-attractive young woman is afforded the dignity and comfort of a change of clothes, a wash, and some food (which she cannot swallow). Her hair is brushed. Her nails are cut. These volunteers, most of whom are sex workers themselves and some of whom are HIV-positive, are keen to show their contempt for the paid staff, for their laziness, cowardice, and heartlessness.

Siem Reap Provincial Hospital, with its single-story blocks and its shaded open ground, is, despite the daytime screeching of its fruit bats, the most peaceful section in the busy center of town, close to the Old Market quarter. But not for long. It has to move elsewhere. The developers have their eyes on it, as they have their eyes on almost every acre of land where they might throw up a cheap hotel, Florida-style—cheap to build that is, and cheap to run. Staff wages—for those applicants who pass an HIV test—are low. But the room rates will be "international" and expressed in U.S. dollars, now the town's semi-official currency, and not in the local riels, which even beggars will refuse. The nearby temples of Angkor built so lovingly a millennium ago are occasioning a rushed and thoughtless epidemic of bed fever—not beds for the sick, of course, but for the target number of fifteen million visitors a year. In 2004 there were just one million tourists for the whole of Cambodia. Already the road out to the airport has become a Via Dollarosa, a dispiriting, vulgar strip where fly-in, fly-out trippers, mostly from Japan, Taiwan, and South Korea, are quarantined and anesthetized against the real Cambodia. Those who do bother to wander in the Old Market quarter will discover not only some of the finest food in Asia and the usual national charm and courtesy, but also legions of amputees, many from Pailin district; tuk-tuk drivers unprepared to take no for an answer; gangs of waifs with their baby siblings as begging accessories; men with anything and everything to sell. All are seagulls to the crust. And all are so skilled at importuning, bullying, and wheedling any visitor who does not simply walk away that in the space of an afternoon I had handed over $8, more than a Cambodian doctor would earn in a week. It seemed to me that I was targeted, because as a male, middle-aged European walking alone, I fit the profile of the sex tourist, of which, on the evidence of the mixed-national, mixed-age, mixed-sized couples on the street, there are many. So, in a country where genuine massages were once part of the culture, I was summoned from the doors of parlors so blatantly "untraditional" that even the words pedicure and reflexology were laden with a new, grubby meaning. I was offered "brides" by shopkeepers. And most alarmingly within plain sight of a street hoarding that declared in English "ABUSE A CHILD IN OUR COUNTRY; GO TO PRISON IN YOURS."

Siem Reap, then, is a town that's being ruined by its closeness to some ruins. Too soon, it will be intolerable, a victim of the Revolution of Rising Expectations, which seems to attach a drawback to every advantage it offers. Its new though selective wealth and modernity seem like an impediment to progress rather than evidence of it. Fortunes will be made, of course, by the already rich and powerful. But there is a maturing poverty of spirit in Siem Reap, and although the foreign visitor will be met with hopeful looks by almost everyone, the hope is only that the visitor will spend. In rural Pailin, though, not once was I requested to give anything. The only demand on me was that I should spend time beneath their roofs to talk, and risk, perhaps, a glass of their rice spirit and some mosquito bites. That remote and backward Cambodia, for all its deprivations and its inequalities, its dangers and its negligence, promises—deserves—a better future than the one being mapped out in the shadows of Angkor. This is the Paradox of Progress.

Here, then, are two Cambodias that offer a health care lottery for its citizens or at least those citizens who cannot afford to pay for private care in Thailand. One is tended by nongovernment organizations such as MSF. Those few Cambodians fortunate enough to live within MSF's specialist orbits can expect treatment as efficient and effective as any offered by hospitals in Europe. The other is, at best, less reliable. Its harshest critics would say that, in a country where each year the same amount—$500 million—is received as official aid as is lost from the economy to corruption, the future is not promising. "What's happening in Cambodia is a mixture of a virtually unregulated private sector, a very badly educated population that doesn't have the capacity to distinguish between good and bad, and a government that is so lowly motivated and unambitious in health care that even when it does spend money it spends it ineffectively," says Bart Janssens, as he contemplates what will happen when MSF withdraws, as it must, from its projects in Pailin and Siem Reap. "The government health service in Pailin has not been able to deal with malaria on its own. So how can we trust their ability to deliver this complicated long-term AIDS treatment on their own? Without external support, I cannot see any sign that they will be able to deliver a worthwhile package of care." There is silence in the room, as no one there can find the energy or evidence to argue that, because of government promises to expand and improve, this judgment is pessimistic and unfair. It is a silence filled with fevers, chills, staring comas, diseases quick to seize their opportunity, and piles of sawdust under unattended beds.

One of many rubbish dumps
that double as a home to
countless people who try to
carve a living out of items
discarded by others.

This woman was in a neglected corner of a state hospital. She was in the final stages of AIDS and seemed to be at death's door. As we stood wondering what, if anything, we could do, five amazing woman arrived in silence from a local NGO that helps sex workers. They scooped her up, cleaned her, clipped her nails, whispered in her ear, squeezed the juice of fresh fruit in her mouth, gently laid her back on a clean bed, and gave her back her dignity. They left as unassumingly as they arrived.

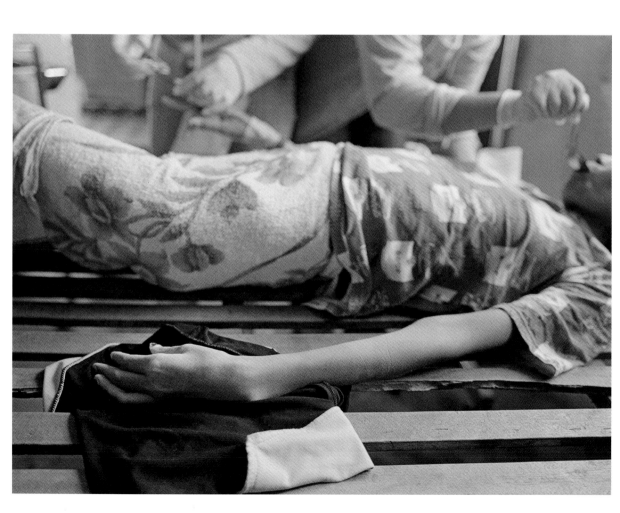

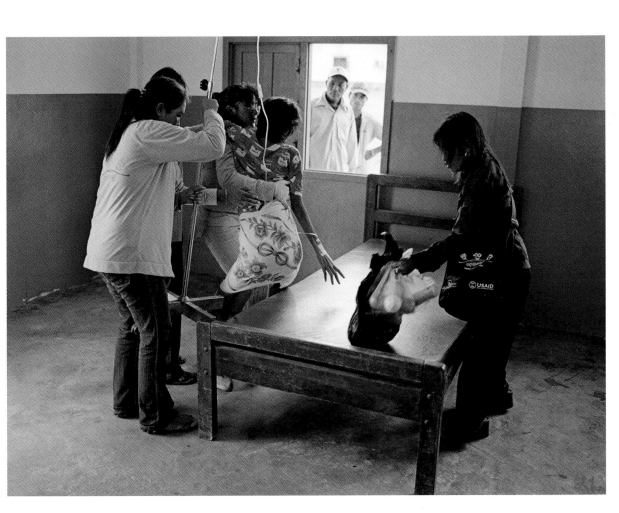

One of the many townships that are constantly threatened by flooding and rampant malaria-bearing mosquitoes.

Chad

The Intolerable and the Unbearable

AA GILL

CHAD IS SPECTACULARLY UNPREPARED for guests.

Accusations of ethnic cleansing and genocide hang in the air, but few with the power to do anything about them want to say the words on record. It's like casting a spell to summon the apocalypse. Once they are said out loud, the world is a step closer to having to confront another Rwanda, another Kosovo. But there is a selective deafness abroad brought about by conflict in the Middle East, Iraq, and the constant sirens of global terrorism, and unstated but ever present is the real-world wisdom that this, after all, is just another Africa story from the continent that brought you all the defining examples of horror; where the usual calibrations of misery don't apply.

Two girls looking through a tent opening. I have no doubt there are dozens of marvelous and edifying things about Chad. Being here is not one of them. Chad, or Tchad as they call it locally, as if named by some passing Yorkshireman, is really no more than a cartographer's patch. The French left it here as somewhere to keep the bottom of the Sahara in, and for those platoons of foreign legionnaires who had the most to forget. It's about the size of Germany, with a population of just nine million. I remember it from my school atlas—it had the lowest per-capita income in the world. It isn't quite the poorest country on Earth anymore, but it is way, way down there: 80 percent of the population lives below the poverty line; 80 percent works the sand. Its primary exports are a handkerchief of cotton, a few cattle, and a near monopoly of the world's gum arabic needs. Gum arabic is essential in the manufacture of good-quality watercolors. Not a lot of people know that; in fact, not a lot of people know anything about landlocked Chad. It has no airline, no railways; it has 33,400 kilometers of road, but only 267 kilometers of them are tarmacked. Life expectancy is forty-eight years, and only if you don't expect much.

It does, though, have a glut of human diversity: two hundred ethnic groups. In the north, the Goran Zaghawa, Kanembou, Ouaddai, Baguirmi, Hadjerai, Fulbe, Kotoko, Hausa, Boulala, and Maba—all Arab and Muslim. In the south are the Moundang, Moussei, and Massa, who are for the most part Christian, which in Africa always comes hyphenated with animist, and they're black. They are the blackest black, blue-black, matt-black black you've ever seen.

Men in the desert sitting in the shade of bush. Chad, along with Sudan, is hung across one of the least reported, potentially most volatile cultural fault lines in the world: the border between black and Arab Africa. Before the Europeans ever arrived there was a history of exploitation, slavery, and massacre. Here, the appellation Muslim or Christian comes with baggage and chains. Chad isn't one of those failed states we hear so much about from smug, overachieving nations: rather it's a stalled state, one that never really made it off the starting blocks of independence. It goes through the stately motions and boasts plenty of initials after its name from international organizations.

It has ambassadors and a billion dollars of debt, it signs international treaties (though I notice it hasn't ratified the international law of the sea yet), but it isn't defined by the niceties of statesmanship. Like Sudan, Chad is a slave to the land on which it precariously squats, earth-blasted and dominated by the sun. This is the hottest place I've ever been. Temperatures are regularly in the fifties (Celsius); they have climbed the thirties before sunrise. This isn't just weather, something mundane to be endured: it's a godlike thing, a shimmering, psychotic, physical presence. It's like living with a bright murderer. Achievement is not measured here, as it is in the damp, green First World, by invention and energy, but by the ability to do as little as possible, for as long as possible, in as much shade as possible.

Chad has three pressing problems. It has the black curse of Africa: unexploited oil. It has the same flag as Romania, and it has between 100,000 and 200,000 refugees. It has gone to the UN to protest about the flag business. To get around, you either hitch a lift on a lorry, hire a four-wheel drive and stutter across the desert, or beg a seat on one of the small humanitarian flights that sustain a skeletal relief effort.

After a couple of days hanging out in the two-story breeze-block and barbed-wire boredom of Ndjamena, we managed to get a flight into the east. At the airport the top-secret French Mirage fighters screamed secretly into the shimmering morning air to spy on North Africa. The French can never actually leave their old colonies. They hang around like gun-toting divorced husbands. We fly to Abéché, which puts up with another French base: legionnaires lounging in the shadows of their Jeeps, sporting nut-hugging camouflage shorts and coquettish little berets. For all their surly élan, they always look like the backup singers for the Village People.

We drive on to Iriba, a town made of mud that rises out of the desert like geometric worm casts. The deafening silence is broken only by the morning throb of the baker's generator and the occasional call of a lovesick donkey. There is nothing to see here, nothing to play at, nothing to talk about, nothing to do, except squat in the shade and throw stones at meager chickens. You can't help but wonder at the terrifying boredom threshold you'd need to call this place home.

Woman with baby on back and child in arms. Iriba has the only hospital for the thousands of refugees stretched across hundreds of miles of border. It's a brick building of three or four little wards and a room that makes do as an operating theater. In the compound are some sagging, dusty tents for the therapeutic feeding of malnourished children, and there is some shade for their mothers and those who have no bed. The hospital is run by Médecins Sans Frontières. Chad has few doctors, and they all work in the capital or for the UN.

There is only one doctor/surgeon, a Belgian girl who looks like she has stepped from a Frans Hals painting; bosomy and blonde, she's like a ghost among her black patients. She dreams Belgian dreams, of dairy products, yogurt, cheese, fountains of milk. She makes her rounds with professional cheerfulness. The sick regard her with that stoic fatalism that is the small dignity of African hospitals. Just having made it here is staggering good fortune.

She stops at the bed of a woman who has given birth to tiny twin boys. They lie like little plucked birds, their bodies flickering with breath. Their mother arranges her shawl to give them shade, gently flicks away the flies, but she won't feed them. She is lactating but she won't feed them. And the hospital won't give them powdered milk because they can't guarantee its supply for the whole of their infancy. It's a standoff.

Twin baby boys. The mother won't or can't say why, one remorseless hour at a time, she can starve her sons to death. She lies apart with an impassive, locked-away beauty, like an odalisque, watching her boys eke out their tiny reserves of existence. The doctor is frustrated. The mother stares, speechlessly daring judgment. The universal blessing of children is for the refugee a curse. How could a lonely girl without a husband or family welcome another pair of mouths, two widow's mites, into this stark, hopeless life? I can only guess at the monstrous ill fortune and misery that led her to this hopeless impasse. She can't kill her babies, as women sometimes do out here in extremis, but she can't help them into her world either, so she lies here silently jammed between the intolerable and the unbearable.

Outside, a thirteen-year-old boy takes painful little steps, helped by an orderly. His brother stepped on the mine that killed him and took this boy's foot, and doctors had to remove one of his testicles. A group of men sitting in the shade give him a little clap. They may be guerrillas: they have bullet and shrapnel wounds; one is paralyzed. Nobody asks.

I stand in on an operation in the little theater. It's hardly sterile. There are sheets over the windows to keep out the desert, but it becomes stifling. Flies hopscotch over the sixteen-year-old girl lying on the table. She has been hit by a truck. They use ketamine as an anesthetic. In the west it is only used as a veterinary drug; here it's a godsend. But while the bone-deep lacerations in the leg are being disinfected, the girl comes around. Her eyes roll with terror, hands jerk, a soft mewing grows to wails, then screams. The nurse reaches for another hypodermic cosh. "I think she'll probably lose this leg," says the doctor.

In the therapeutic feeding center, children are given high-protein porridge; mothers and grandmothers finger-feed tiny mouthfuls into slowly ruminating mouths. These children, with their stretched-parchment faces, sparse hair, and huge, sorrowful eyes, are always shocking, and I am aware of the irony of how ancient, wise, and calm starving children always look.

A woman rocks a spindly, floppy toddler. He is dying, she says. And closes his eyes. "No," explains a nurse through an interpreter. "He's very dehydrated. He will die if they don't get fluids into him." She adds that the mother shouldn't have taken out the saline drip they put into his arm. She tries to fit another, but the mother pushes it away; no, she insists, her child is dead. The nurses, though compassionate in a matter-of-fact way, get grittily frustrated at the lack of understanding in these mothers. Medicine is so second nature to us, yet so mythical to them.

There is a little albino lad about two years old who is everyone's favorite. They call him Petit Blanc. He is responding well to the therapeutic feeding, the wrinkled skin filling out and dimpling. "He won't last long," she says. "They never do, albinos. Skin cancer." Does his mother know? "She does now. I told her." Can't she do anything? The doctor shrugs: "Keep him out of the sun." But all this woman has between her and the blistering, baby-murderous sky is a thin veil. "You see, already he has the melanomas."

About an hour away from the hospital, past dead tanks, relics of a defunct civil war, is the desert refugee camp of Iridimi. Built for 6,000, it sags under the needs of 14,000 souls who live beneath plastic sheets and rags stretched over thorn trees. Each day brings more lorries laden with Sudanese blacks and their bright bundles of belongings.

Refugee camp. The gunships that make up the Sudanese air force drop handmade bombs on border towns. The war in Darfur is being pursued by the last irregular cavalry still plying their trade: the Janjaweed. On horses and camels, they surround black villages. They are supported by regular army troops. The Sudanese government denies involvement, claiming they are local gangs. The Janjaweed live by looting cattle, grain, small amounts of cash and slaves.

The government's reason for not intervening is clear: it's ethnic cleansing and genocide. There is meant to be a UN-monitored ceasefire, but the casualties, terrified women and starving children, still stream across the border. The refugees' stories have a metronomic repetition: their villages are shelled or bombed, the Janjaweed surround them and kill all the men and boys old enough to be remotely threatening. They systematically rape the women, taking some as slaves; they then burn the villages and the crops they can't steal, and ride off the livestock. And still the government claims the Janjaweed have nothing to do with them.

Khartoum offers access to the international community to check these calumnies, these accusations. Anyone can come to see that really Sudan is lovely—a hot Switzerland with mosques—but invariably the promised visas for observers and NGOs never materialize. If they do manage to get one, access to the worst areas is limited. There are five hundred applications from humanitarian agencies alone gathering diplomatic dust. This pattern of denial and opaque promises of transparency is familiar after twenty years of war in the south. Who is going to do anything about it? Who will stand up to the Janjaweed? They are among the most feared, sadistically ruthless, irregular thugs in a continent glutted with military horror.

Women in the desert. Anyone who doubts that this conflict is either genocidal or ethnically motivated only has to visit these camps. All the refugees are black; there are no Arabs here. And even more shocking, 90 percent of them are women and children. The children up to the age of five are about fifty-fifty girls and boys, as you'd expect. From five to fifteen they are 70 percent girls. Some of the men would have stayed to fight or hide with their livestock but, as Sherlock Holmes used to say, "when you have eliminated the impossible, whatever remains . . . must be the truth." It is impossible to imagine any other explanation for this disappeared generation of men than systematic murder. The women tell of deaths, terrified flight, lost children, missing husbands. "We will never go back," says one. "Unless the UN have soldiers, and only if they are white soldiers," adds another.

The refugees are related linguistically and tribally to the Chadians on this side of the border; they have moved and traded together for hundreds of years, and are now welcomed. It is humbling to see with what good grace the people with the least offer shelter and succor to those with nothing. The majority of refugees are not in the rich First World, but in the poorest bits of the Third World, where they and their hosts grow poorer.

Women collecting water in the desert. The greatest problem after safety is water. From sunrise to sunset in the camp, a long line of women wait under the deathly sun to fill containers from a couple of standpipes that are fed by large plastic bladders, which in turn are filled by lorries. I have to drink at least six liters of soupy water a day to stop my tongue cracking and my throat closing up.

But I never see these women drink. Their bright cotton shawls flap in the wind, revealing a little arm or resting head tied to a back. In the white light, the rivers of cloth look like spinnakers of saturated color, printed with the repeated pictures of other people's good fortune. You see Mercedes badges and BMW signs, footballs, mobile phones, airplanes, the faces of politicians who've promised prosperity, cities of skyscrapers—the ragged incantations for an unavailable life, and the shaming irony of a desperate African version of designer labels. Here is a picture of a house you would be happy in, a diploma you could get if there was a school, a car, a comfy chair. Impossible, ridiculous cotton dreams of a fantasy luxury.

Woman sitting in the desert surrounded by water containers. A mile or so outside the camp, in a stand of knotted acacias, is an ancient, stone-lined well, one of the Sahara's fabled oases. It doesn't look like the painting. A dirty, shit-strewn muddy quag, where herdsmen sweat and slither at the heavy job of tending their xylophone-ribbed flocks. They perch precariously on the edge of the well; the thick water at the bottom is only a few feet deep. In the bed of the wadi there is a stinking, half-burned pyre of donkey and goat corpses. The desert is littered with animal cadavers; elsewhere, parched livestock stand in little bits of filigreed shade and wait to die. The sun desiccates their bodies to tough bags, leather and bones that grin at the sky. For some reason there are no carrion eaters, no vultures, so the dead lie around like old teabags. When the rains do come, they'll become slimy and get washed into the wells and wadis, and leach into the water table. The risk of a cholera epidemic is just one runny, squatting child away.

The desert and the water won't support the Chadians and the Sudanese refugees, and there are signs that the welcome is growing thin. Charities drilling in search of new wells for permanent camps have been angrily stopped by farmers.

We drive on a spine-fusing, hip-dislocating, brain-poaching journey to Tine, a market town that crosses the border. It sits on one of the skeletal lines of trade and communication that bleach into the Sahara. The route down from Libya meets a crossroads from Sudan into Central Africa here. The border itself is no more than a dry wadi and some trees, under which sit a squad of Chadian soldiers. There are a couple of impressive mosques and a large covered market. Prices are astronomic for the bits and boxes of white goods that made the Homeric saga through the desert to end up here.

Across the dry river and the shade trees you see the other half of town, the Sudanese half, a mirror image of mud brick and minaret, utterly deserted, where not a soul, not a donkey exists. It's a town that's suffered a stroke: one half paralyzed, the other bereft

95

and staggering. The Janjaweed came, murdered, and expelled the left-hand population. People ask, how could the Sudanese do this to their own people? I've heard Sudanese spokesmen with honey voices rhetorically ask the same thing. "Why would we do these things to our own people?" The answer would seem to be that the Arab-Muslim regime in Khartoum doesn't consider the black inhabitants of their southern and eastern regions as their people, their kin, at all.

With its rigid, prescriptive interpretation of sharia, Khartoum attempted to develop chemical and nuclear weapons. It was Khartoum that sheltered Osama Bin Laden and Al-Qaeda while they planned the embassy bombing in Nairobi and Dar es Salaam. Khartoum pursued a civil war in the south for twenty years, engineering famine as a weapon of mass murder. And it still accepts the oldest, most inhuman of mass crimes: slavery. Blacks are captured, kept, bred, and ransomed as slaves. This is a blatantly racist, genocidal regime. The UN has called the catastrophe in Darfur the worst humanitarian disaster in the world, but that's a euphemism. It describes a consequence, not the cause. This is a calculated crime. The greatest inhumanitarian disaster in the world.

Women and children in the desert. In another refugee camp a boy, perhaps twenty, approaches me. He is wearing a once-smart sports jacket and trousers and—a rare thing—spectacles. "You speak English?" he asks. "I was a student of English in Darfur at the university. I was in my second year." He looks around the ragged shelters. "This is a bad place, very bad. We need two things: water and an English department."

I think he means it as a joke; it's a bleakly funny line. But he is absolutely serious. He is close to tears and I understand what a struggle it must have been to get to university at all, what a monumental investment, not just for him but his family, his village, this slightly bookish boy in his western charity clothes and wise glasses, already approaching statistical middle age, cast out as homeless, begging flotsam among a diaspora of grieving women. It is such a pitiful waste.

On the long, dry road home, I stop off at the hospital in Iriba. The woman who'd pronounced her son dead has had her prophecy fulfilled. The war-wounded men come and bury the little bundle in the graveyard behind the latrines. She sits hunched, facing the wall. She doesn't cry. I haven't seen one of these women cry. Inside, the mother has begun feeding her twin boys, her reasons for offering the m life as secretly implacable as had been her decision to withhold it.

This tree had been planted on the hospital grounds. Like everything in Chad, it was struggling against the unbearable heat.

One of many dead donkeys.
Without water, nothing
survives for long in the heat.

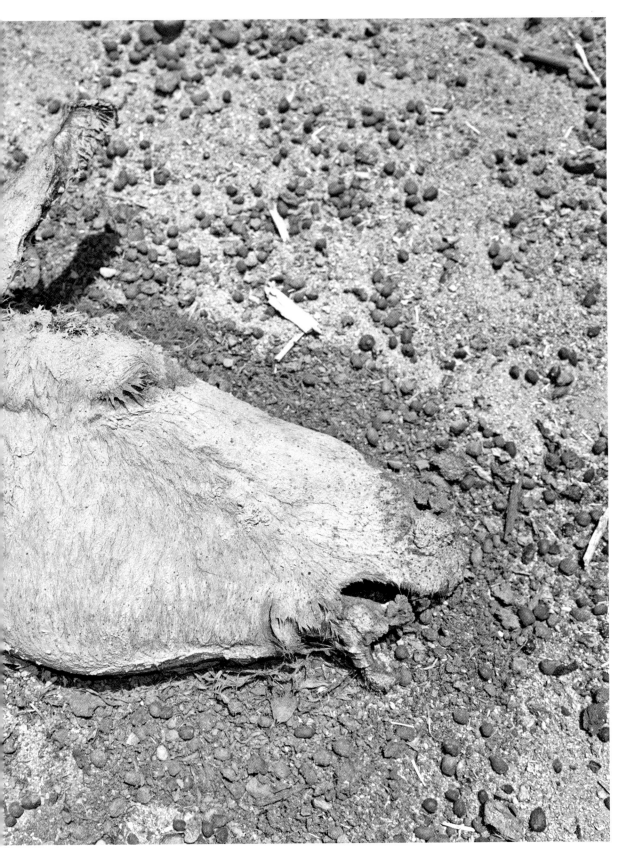

Left: Just over the border from Sudan, women queue for hours in the blistering heat. This is not a normal population on the move: all the men and boys are missing, either killed by or fighting against the Janjaweed. It is a portrait of war.

Below: After an epic cross-border journey on foot, these women finally arrived at the makeshift MSF clinic, sheltering their children from the heat and dust as well as they could.

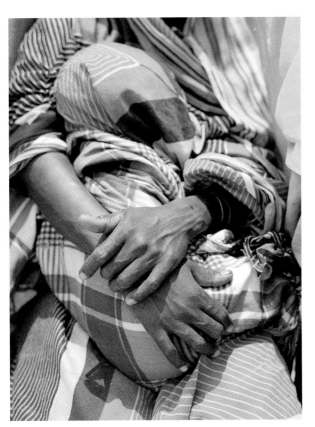

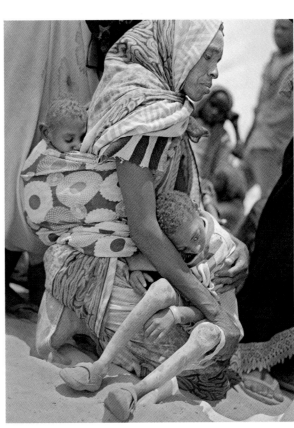

The material used for the emergency tents and clinics provides some shelter from the scorching sun outside.

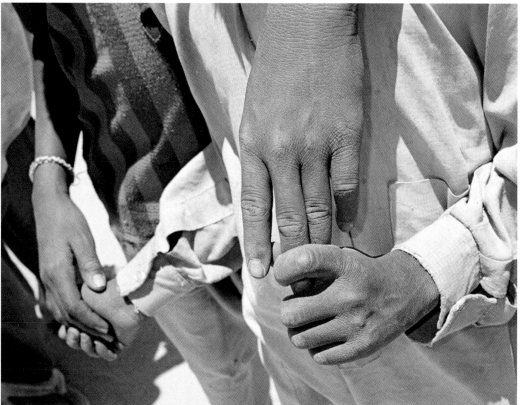

Left: Scenes from the refugee camp.

Below: This woman had recently given birth to twin boys but did not seemingly have the strength or resources to feed both.

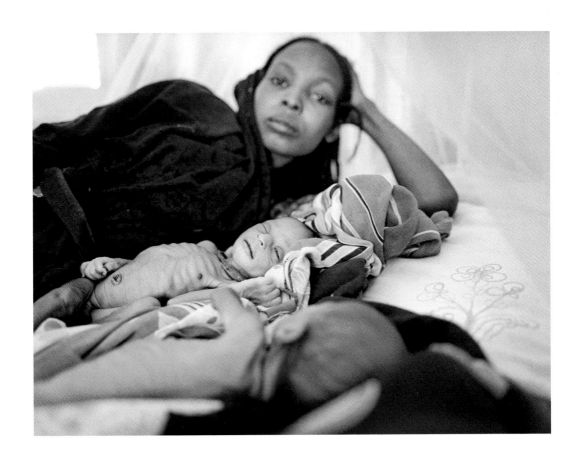

Cali, Colombia

The Return of Death

MARTIN AMIS

1. Exit wound

It was a *bala perdida* that almost did it for little Kevin: the stray
bullet went in through his nape and came out through his brow.
That was a year ago, when he was four. The incident took place a few
yards from where we now sat, in a front room that felt like a carless
garage, with its damp, cement floor, and a series—almost a pattern—
of scorched light fixtures along its walls and ceiling. Kevin's
grandmother runs a modest line in secondhand clothes; there
was a stretched wire with some coat hangers on it, and a plastic
bag stuffed with espadrilles and flip-flops. The family dog, small,
frazzled, and elderly, was still growling at us after half an hour, even
while scratching its ear with a raised hind paw. Kevin was playing
in the street when the car sped by (it never became clear to me what,
if anything, the *muchachos* were trying to hit). At the hospital, his
twenty-year-old mother was told that Kevin had five minutes to live.
They operated, and, after a five-day coma, a silent and unsmiling
spell in a wheelchair, and a course of rehabilitation, Kevin seems
to have reemerged as a confident, even stylish little boy. Kevin was
deeply withdrawn for months; he responded only listlessly to other
children and was indifferent to adults. When he divided his toy
soldiers into good guys and bad guys, the bad guys always won.

What happened to Kevin was an accident: an accident in a
very accident-prone city, but an accident. Another child, ten-
year-old Bryan, will find it harder to gain the (in fact nonexistent)
consolation of "closure." He was shot in the back by his best friend.
Bryan's offense? It wasn't as if he threatened to take his football
home—all he did was say he didn't want to play anymore. Bryan
now has a palsied gate (a slow, bobbing hop) and a face deprived
of symmetry; and he looks blind, too (though he isn't), because his
gaze seeks nothing. Kevin, on the other hand, amiably complied
when his grandmother, parting his hair and lifting his fringe,
showed me the entry wound, the exit wound; they looked like
vaccination scars. As we took our leave, the dog gave us an eloquent
farewell snarl: good riddance to bad rubbish. The dog, it seemed,
had taken on the fear and distrust that ought to belong to Kevin.

In the forecourt of the house opposite, a fully adult male
(statistically quite a rarity in this neighborhood) was closing up
his house for the night; he stared at us with frank but nonspecific
hostility, all the while rearranging the contents of his crimson
running shorts. Some residents try to disguise it with fancy grilles
and lattices, but most of the houses, in non-downtown Cali, are
wholly encaged. The male adult, across the street, now proceeded
to wall himself up in his personal penitentiary. In El Distrito, the
boys rage all night and sleep all day (in their coffins and crypts);
and at dusk they all turn into vampires.

We always had to be out by five—but wait. There was still time to visit Ana Milena. Some years ago her sister was paralyzed after being shot in the throat by a neighbor; she died of depression and self-starvation in 1997. Seven years later, Ana Milena broke up with her *novio*. So he attacked her in broad daylight at a bus stop, stabbing her in the navel, in the neck, and twice in the head. Their daughter (then nearly three) stood and watched, and then hid her face. She still insists that her mother was hit by a car.

Gang slang for a homemade gun is *una pacha*: a baby's bottle. The violence starts at once and never goes away. Kevin's scars are not at all disfiguring. He has an entry wound and an exit wound. His was easily the most hopeful story I heard in Cali. In general, you suspect, emotionally and psychologically there may be entry wounds, but there are no exit wounds.

2. La Esperanza
Occupying about a quarter of Colombia's third city, Aguablanca (Whitewater) consists of about 130 barrios; each barrio has two or three gangs, and all the gangs are theoretically at war with all the others. What do they fight about? They don't fight about drugs (ecstasy and dope are popular, but the cocaine trade is an elite activity). They fight about turf (a corner, a side street); they fight about anything at all to do with disrespect (what might be called "eyebrow" murders); and they fight about the fight that went before (*venganza* operates like a series of chain letters). Yet the main fuel of the murder figures, here as elsewhere, is the fantastic plenitude of weaponry. A homemade gun costs just over £20, a hand grenade just over £12 (a hand grenade is what you'll be needing if, for instance, you gatecrash a party and get turned away). "Guns don't kill people. People kill people," argued Ronald Reagan. You could take this line further, and say that guns don't kill people. Bullets kill people. In Cali they cost fifty cents each and can be sold to minors individually, like cigarettes.

Three teenage girls, acting as the representatives of a barrio called El Barandal (The Rail), advised us not to enter; but a couple of hundred yards down the road, at La Esperanza (Hope), we were casually welcomed. I asked Roger what had made the difference, and he said that El Barandal was even poorer and dirtier and, crucially, fuller; there was more humiliation, more wrath, and more guns. Sara, the friendliest of the Esperanzans, had a different emphasis: *"Somos todos negros, y somos buena gente."*

"We're all black, and we're good people." And good people they would need to be. Every South American country has its own name for places like this. In Bogotá the word is *tugurio* (hovel), but the Chilean version best evokes La Esperanza: *callampa* (mushroom). "Whitewater" suggests a fast-flowing river, or rapids. The marshlands, where the barrios sprouted up in the 1980s, are now whitened by their own putrefaction. The endless ditch isn't deep enough to submerge the tubs and tyres that disturb its caustic mantle. Yet the egrets still consider it worth their while to paddle in it and peck in it; when they flap their wings you expect them to fly off on half-corroded stilts.

The people here are *desplazados*, displaced peasants, mainly from the Pacific coast of the country. Cali contains about 70,000 of the displaced. Some are pushed from the land by that irresistible modern force, urbanization; others are fleeing what may be the final convulsions of a spasm civil war that began in 1948. But here they are, with no money and no jobs. Colombia does not provide free health care or free education for its citizens; and the first explanation you reach for here is the enormous South American lacuna—taxation. Taxation, necessarily of the rich, is simply not enforced. To paraphrase ex-president Lleras Camargo: Latin Americans have gone to jail for many strange reasons, but not one, in the whole continent, has ever gone to jail for tax fraud.

Of the four houses I ducked into at La Esperanza, Sara's, counterintuitively, was easily the worst. Your first step took you onto a nail bed of chipped, upward-pointing tiles on bare soil: this was clearly a work in progress, but for a moment it felt like a booby trap. Then a communal area, and a dorm of crushed cots. Then, finally, out toward the water, a kitchen/bathroom, with lots of exposed (and ingenious) plumbing, a hotplate, a heap of compost in the corner, and a largely ornamental fridge with four eggs in its open door. A huge negress, already stripped to the waist, pushed past us and disappeared into a wooden wigwam. There came a gush of water and a burst of song.

Outside, the ladies laugh and playfully squabble about whose house is the prettiest. La Esperanza's lone shop has only a handwritten sign on its door, saying *no fio* (no credit) and sells only tobacco and starch, but the residents call it their *supermercado*. As for the rancid water, into which the barrio seems about to collapse, you just tell yourself, said Sara, that it's a nice sea view.

Colombia has a foot in both of the two great oceans. It also straddles the equator. At noon on a clear day, your shadow writhes around your shoes like a cat. We paid our visit on one of the cooler mornings (the clouds were the same color as the water), and it was onerous to imagine the barrio under a sky-filling sun. Just back down the road, at the entry point to Aguablanca, the smell of the blighted canal, with its banks of solid rubbish, grips you by the tonsils. This smell is La Esperanza's future.

3. Stag night

The classic *venganza*, in Cali gangland, is not a bullet through the head but a bullet through the spine. Some thought has gone into this. "One month after the attack," says Roger Micolta, the young therapist from Médecins Sans Frontières, "the victims ask me, 'Will I ever walk?' Two months after, they ask me, 'Will I ever fuck?'" The answer to both questions is almost invariably *no*. So the victims not only have to live with their wound; they have to wear it, they have to wheel it. Everybody knows that they have lost what made them men.

At the municipal hospital in Aguablanca, at therapy time in the mid-afternoons, crippled innocents, like limping Bryan, are outnumbered by crippled murderers—by cripples who have done much crippling in their time. They go through interminable sets of exercises: pull-ups, sideways rolls. Girlfriends and sisters take hairbrushes to their legs, to encourage sensation. One young man, inching along the parallel bars, keeps freezing and closing his eyes in helpless grief. Another has a weight strapped to his ankle; he is watched by his mother, who reflexively swings her own leg in time with his.

In the back room there is a storyboard used for psychosexual counseling. *"Lo mas frustrante: estar impotente. No poder sentir, no comprension, no tener ganas."* To be unable to feel, to understand, to have no desire. The MSF educational posters, too, rightly and aggressively zero in on the question of testosterone. A typical specimen shows a pistol with its shaft curling into a droop: "To carry a gun doesn't make you a man." Another shows a series of waistbands with the gun positioned behind the belt buckle and pointing straight downward. In Cali, all the stuff you have ever read or heard about male insecurity, phallic symbols, and so on, is almost tediously verified, everywhere you look.

Nearby, in the market streets, the shops are disconcertingly full of goods, essentials, and nonessentials—cheap cameras, exercise gear, a chemist selling Shower Organizers (an item badly needed in La Esperanza). The armless, headless mannequins are faithful to the indigenous female type: high and prominent backsides, hefty breasts with nipples the size of drawer pulls. At the patisserie there is an elaborate cake representing a thonged *muchacha*. Another represents a penis. The testicles are hirsute with squiggles of chocolate; the blancmange-hued helmet bears a thin swipe of cream, appreciatively indicating the slit. A hen-night item, you might suppose. The inscription says, *"Chupame, carino,"* in a toilingly decorative hand. Suck me, honey. There is no female form for it in Spanish—no *carina*. But you wonder. In Cali, maybe the tackle cake is intended for the stags.

111

That night there was a cookout on a rooftop downtown. The guests were professionals, academics; there was music and some dancing—very chaste and technical. Yet even here a sexual trapdoor can open up beneath you. At one point a young woman began an innocent conversation with a handsome young guest, and after some joking in male undertones she was grinningly handed a paper napkin. The suggestion was that she would now be able to wipe away her drool.

All the outer walls around us were topped by shards of glass, varying dramatically in size, shape, and thickness. If glass-topped walls constitute a kind of architecture, then here we had it in its Gothic phase. In Britain this form of crime prevention was a very frequent (and very stimulating) sight in my childhood—but not in my youth. Again and again you kept vaguely thinking: two or three generations, forty or fifty years—that's how far back they are. Just now, Colombia seems to be poised to turn in the right direction. If there is a current theme in the evolution of South America, it appears to be this: the vested interests (very much including the United States) are tolerating an improvement in the caliber of the political leaders, with Kirchner in Argentina, Lula in Brazil, and now, perhaps, Uribe in Colombia.

Beyond the sliver-studded walls you could see an entire mountainside of lights. This was the *callampa* of Siloe, which, I am told, is roughly twice as violent as Aguablanca.

4. *The central divide*

We were on the central divide of the dual carriageway, about three hundred yards from one of the most decidedly no-go barrios. Three *muchachos* approached. When I offered Marlboros I got two takers; they lowered their heads as they smoked, embarrassed by the fact that they didn't inhale. The third boy declined. He didn't say, *"No fumo";* he said, *"No puedo fumar."* It wasn't that he didn't smoke. He couldn't smoke (much as he'd like to). Then he lifted his T-shirt and showed us why.

His right shoulder, his right breast, and his right armpit, where he had recently been shot, formed an unmade bed of bandages and brown, sticky tape. He had recently been stabbed, too, and with a vengeance. From his sternum to his navel ran the wound, not yet a scar, pink and plump, like a garden worm. He turned out to be a patient of Roger's (one of the less tractable). His name was John Anderson. This was by no means the first time he had been shot, nor the first time he had been stabbed. He was sixteen.

Like everyone else the boys were keen to be photographed, but first they had to go and get their weapon. After rooting around in a rubbish dump across the road, they returned with a sawn-off shotgun. John Anderson posed, with his flintlock, his knife wound (like an attempt at vertical seppuku), his stupidly wonky hairstyle, his trigger-happy stare. Abruptly you were struck by the thinness and inanity of it: an existence so close to nonexistence. It couldn't have been clearer that John Anderson had weeks to live.

To say this of human beings is to say both the best and the worst. They can get used to *anything*.

5. *The not-so-interesting crippled murderer*

I got used to it too. You find yourself thinking: if I had to live in El Distrito, I wouldn't stay at Kevin's but at Ana Milena's where they have cable TV and that nice serving hatch from the kitchen to the living room. And if I had to live in La Esperanza, I would gently but firmly refuse Sara's offer and try to buy myself into the place four houses along, where the guy has the fridge and the fan (and the ten dependents). Similarly, I now found myself thinking: you know, this crippled murderer isn't nearly as interesting as the crippled murderer I interviewed the day before yesterday. And so it seemed. Raul Alexander was nothing much, compared to Mario.

When we called, Raul was lying on his bed watching *The Simpsons*. In Kevin's house, in Ana Milena's house, in Sara's house, there were never any young men. When there is a young man in the house, it's because he can't walk away from it. He will certainly be a cripple, and very probably a crippled murderer.

With his buzz-cut hair and his ingenious little face, Raul looked like the kind of waiter you might grow fond of at a resort hotel. It sounds tactless, but the truth was that we were *settling* for Raul. We had hoped for Alejandro. He was the crippled murderer who couldn't get to sleep at night if he hadn't killed someone earlier that day. But we'd already skipped an appointment with Alejandro, more than once, and when we did appear his mother told us he had taken the dog to the vet. Was this a particularly savage Latino anathema, or just a weak excuse? I thought of the gang verb, *groseriar* (*no respetar*). And it was a relief, in the end, to make do with Raul.

Asked about his childhood, he described it as normal, which it seemed to be, except for a father who remained in situ well into Raul's teens. He started stealing car parts, then cars, then cars with people sitting inside them. "One on Monday, one on Thursday." Then he got competitive with a friend: there would now be six armed carjackings a day. He started stealing money that was on its way to or from shops, factories, banks. He did nine months in prison and emerged predictably fortified. By now the bank deliveries were oversubscribed, with queues of blaggers in the street; so Raul started venturing within. These weekly capers were not to last. He did thirty months, came out for three days, and went back in for three years. During his last stretch Raul killed a man, for the first time, he claimed: payback for a stabbing.

Blooded, his bones made, Raul took a job in an office. That last sentence may look slightly odd to a non-Caleno, but when someone around here says that "they worked in an office" or did "office work," you know exactly what they did: they sat by a phone, on retainer (£250 a month), and did targeted assassinations through an agent for a further £100 a time. Boys who work in offices, incidentally, are not called "office boys," so far as I know, but boys are valued in office work, because they are cheap, fearless, and unimprisonable until the age of eighteen. Raul would have been in his twenties at this stage. John Anderson, though, for example—he may well have worked in an office. The most popular day for office murders in Cali is Sunday: that's when people are more likely to be found at home.

Raul's downfall? By this point my faith in his veracity, or in his self-awareness, never high, began to dwindle. How did he tell it? He had some trouble with a guy who shot his cousin, a murder that a friend of his (Raul's) impulsively avenged. There was this consignment of marijuana . . . Raul circled and meandered, and it all seemed to come down to a *problema*, a poker game, a spilled drink—an "eyebrow" *venganza*.

We took our leave of Raul Alexander heartlessly early (one of us had to get to the airport), and filed through a sunny nook containing his wheelchair and his walker. When, minutes earlier, I asked him how many people he had killed, he pouted and shrugged and said, *"Ocho?"* You thought: oh, sure. But even if Raul was dividing his score by two, or by ten, he was nothing much, compared to Mario.

6. Mario

He too is lying on his bed, apparently naked but for a pale blue towel spread over his waist. The reproductions on the wall of the adjacent sitting room—a wooden cottage near a waterfall, a forest with a white horse picked out by opalescent sunbeams— prompt you, in describing Mario, to seek the heroic frame. You think of the fallen Satan, hurled over the crystal battlements. Mario was once very radiant and dynamic, but he has made the journey from power to no power, and now he lies on his bed all day with his clicker and his Cartoon Network.

Although the long legs are tapering and atrophying, Mario's upper body still proudly ripples. The armpits, in particular, are unusually pleasing; they look shaved or waxed, but a glance at the half-naked relative in the kitchen, who has his hands clasped behind his head, confirms that the abbreviation is natural. Mario's trouble, his difficulty, begins with his face. With its close-set eyes divided by a shallow bridge, its very strong jaw (full of avidity and appetite), Mario's is the face of a mandrill. If you'd seen Raul Alexander coming for you on the street, in a bar, or standing in your doorway, you would have tried to resist him, or reason with him, or reimburse him. If you'd seen Mario coming for you, in his prime, you wouldn't have done anything at all.

As a seven-year-old, he hid under a cloth-covered table and listened, while nine other peasants, two of them women, killed his father. Mario is about thirty now: this would have happened during the period known as La Violencia (though there is barely a period of Colombian history that could not be so called). When he was twelve he made a start on his *venganzas*, killing the first of the nine peasants with a knife. He then went on to kill the other eight. Then he gravitated to Cali. That's who they are in Aguablanca, in Siloe: peasants, and now the children of peasants, drastically citified.

After a spell in carjacking, then in kidnapping (a vast field), Mario was called up for military service. On his discharge he took his improved organizational skills and "went to the woods," supervising the production and transfer of *talco* (cocaine) in rural Colombia and in Equador. This was itself a kind of military tour; your adversary was not the police but the army. Mario speaks of his time in the woods with fondness and awe. "The cocaine came in blocks, all of them stamped—very pretty (*muy bonita*), how it shines (*como brilla*). Once I saw a *whole room* full of money."

He came back to Cali equipped with discipline, esprit, and (one imagines) a ton of pesos, and started "enjoying life." It is not hard to imagine Mario enjoying life: in a city full of terrifying men, he would have been universally feared. He took a job in an office, and in this capacity he killed about 150 people in six years. But that's a lot of *venganza* to be storing up, and in December 2003 they came for him in force. He was at a stoplight when four men on two motorbikes pulled up on either side of the car.

Now Mario's sister served coffee—a profound improvement on the Tizer and Dandelion & Burdock you are usually offered in Colombia. (It seems deeply typical of Aguablanca that there is never any coffee; you trudge from place to place searching for a cup.) Time to go. I asked Mario to describe the difference between his first murder and his last, and he said, "The first, with the knife? It was awful. I had bad dreams. I cried all day. I had paranoia. But the last time? *Nada*. You just think: and now I get paid."

Mario called for his cloudy trophies and lay half-immersed in them: his handgun (very heavy—to its wielder it must have the divine heaviness of gold), his X-rays (the lucent second bullet in the arched thorax), and his stainless police record (which cost him £750). He also had his clicker, his clock, and, of course, his transparent wallet of urine taped to the side of the bed.

They are still after Mario, so it was double deliverance to get out of his house. When I thought about it later, though, it seemed to me that Mario, with his provenance, was entitled to his hate; and that the non-monstrous Raul Alexander, with his slight frame and his bellhop's smile, was the more representative figure: a leaf in the wind of the peer group. Machismo, in its Latin American mutation, has one additional emphasis, that of indifference—unreachable indifference. You felt that indifference very strongly with John Anderson, on the central divide. Any kind of empathy is not just enfeebling—it is effeminate. You have no empathy even for yourself. So it appears that the Aguablancans are playing a children's game—kids' stuff—of dare and taunt and posture, in which they all feel immortal. Except that the sticks and stones are now knives and guns and hand grenades.

As you drive back into the city, you see boys—jugglers—performing for an audience sitting trapped in its cars. They are not juggling with clubs or oranges but with machetes and brands of fire.

7. The return of death

On my last day I went to the MSF exhibition of photographs and case histories. There were familiar names and familiar faces—Ana Milena, little Kevin. On the night the exhibition opened, all the featured victims attended, except Edward Ignacio. Still recovering from his multiple panga wounds, Edward Ignacio was shot dead earlier that day.

From there I went to the cemetery in the middle of town, a small and crowded plot of land between the football ground and the busy Texaco. The entrance was almost submerged by road works: a steamroller, a cement mixer (with its dedicated generator), and hillocks of hot tar. Here, tradesmen had gathered with sustaining soft drinks and ice creams. A storm was coming, and you could smell the moisture in the dust.

The cemetery was more like a morgue than a graveyard, with the dead stacked into a series of thick blocks, each berth the size of a paving stone. Every panel had something written on it, at the minimum just the name and the year of interment, in magic marker; others were far more elaborate, with framed photographs, poems, avowals (*"yo te quiero"*), figurines, crosses, hearts, angels.

We had come with a woman named Marleny Lopez. Her husband was one of the few who had been buried in the earth. The tombstone gave his name and dates, Edinson Mora, 1965–1992. But this was an engraver's error. Edinson was in fact thirty-seven when he died, two years ago. He was playing dominoes with a policeman, and he won. This was perhaps survivable; but then the loser had to pay for the beers.

Most of the other dates, when given fully, were shorter than Edinson's: 1983–2001, 1991–2003. On the whole they got longer as you moved deeper in and further back in time. This one, a century— but this one, eight months. Further back in time, too, the names ceased to be Anglophone (no Kevins and Bryans). And so went Diesolina, Arcelio, Hortencia, Bartolome, Nieves, Santiago, Yolima, Abelardo, Luz, Paz, and so on.

I returned from one of the back alleys and found myself in the middle of a burial service. There was a coffin, with four bearers, and well over a hundred people had come to mourn. This wasn't a gang slaying, a drive-by, a *bala perdida*. A woman had died of a heart attack at the age of twenty-eight: 1976–2004. What happened next happened suddenly. I had spent the recent days making believe that death didn't matter. Now a bill was presented to me for this laxity. It was a chastisement to see the bitter weeping of the husband, the bitter weeping of the mother. It was a chastisement, and one long overdue, to see death reassuming its proper weight.

Below: A gunshot victim.

Right: John Anderson was only sixteen when one of the neighboring gangs virtually disemboweled him. To their surprise he survived, and when they heard he was out of the hospital they shot him. His torso was his own archaeology of violence.

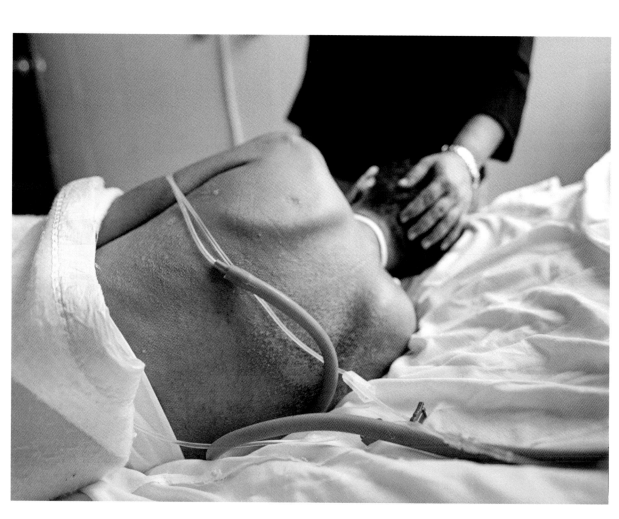

Farfetched fictional characters could not compare with Mario's life story. As a seven-year-old he hid beneath the tablecloth of his kitchen as a gang of nine murdered his parents. By the time he was twelve he had killed the first of the gang and by sixteen he had killed them all with a knife. Already numb, he went on to assassinate a further 150 men in six years. Eventually they caught up with him and shot him in the spine.

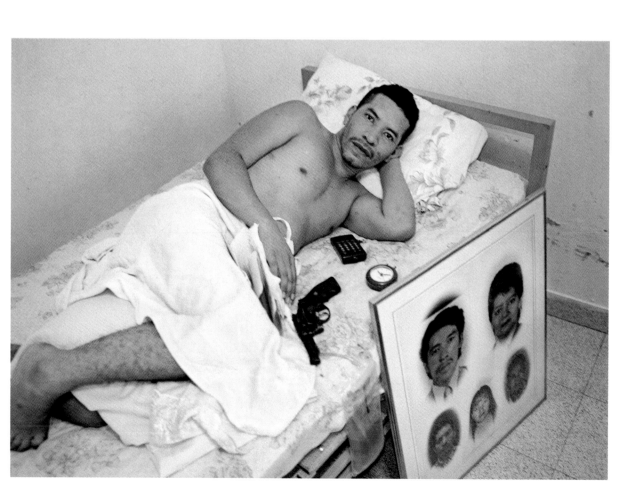

A religious icon in the MSF
care center.

With so much gun crime and instant reprisals, even the hospitals in Cali are dangerous places. This is one of the prisonlike gates at the state hospital.

The streets of Cali.

Colombia sometimes felt like the Wild West, with talk of gun battles and shootouts in the streets daily. Then out of nowhere this man appeared, a macho man who could only be described as joyriding his horse through the streets of the favela.

Congo-Brazzaville

Quietly in Hope

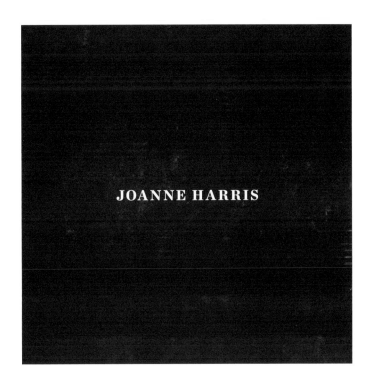

JOANNE HARRIS

I AWAKE EARLY to the sound of drumming and clapping from the nearby church. There are hundreds of churches in Brazzaville, with services throughout the day and night. In daylight Brazzaville seems more than ever a crossroads between worlds: bombed-out buildings stand alongside elegant glass towers; suited businessmen mix with ragged street children; expensive European cars with the battered and psychedelic taxis that constitute 90 percent of the city's traffic.

We drive out of the city in land cruisers toward Ngangalingolo, on the outskirts of Brazzaville. Since October 2002, thousands of displaced and destitute people fleeing the fighting in the Pool region have ended up here, living in crowded camps and subsisting on whatever they can forage.

The Pool region, once known as the "breadbasket of the Congo," has suffered most from the war. Formerly a prosperous area, rich in cattle and agriculture, it has been devastated by conflict between the government and the Ninja rebels.

The women in the food queue approach us. Behind their concern, their dignity, lies an overwhelming need to tell their stories. My name is Julienne. She is in her thirties, with a worn, still-beautiful face, and has clearly dressed in her very best clothes to come to the hospital. I'm a widow, with four children. My husband was killed during the war. Last October, soldiers came to our village. I don't know which army they were from. They take off their uniforms and come back as civilians, so no one knows who they are. In any case, it doesn't matter. These soldiers had machine guns and machetes and torches. They knocked on our doors in the middle of the night, demanding money. When we told them we didn't have any, they took some of the little girls away and raped them. I asked God to help us, but He didn't.

For two months Julienne and the other villagers hid in the forest, foraging for food as helicopters passed overhead. At last, they decided to risk the dangerous three-day journey to this camp.

I ask Julienne if she will go home, now the crisis is over. Home to what? There's nothing left. Soldiers burnt the village—took everything, even the bricks. There's peace now, so they tell us. But that's what they told us last time.

We drive farther down the road to Kinkala, where the military is a large and inescapable presence. On the way to the hospital a truck filled with weapons and soldiers passes by. A soldier fixes us with a tripod-mounted machine gun as we stand on the grassy verge, makes childish poof-ing noises with his mouth. Jenny, the English doctor at the hospital, assures us that the soldiers are not usually troublesome. They are short of food, however, and their wages haven't been paid for some time. At the end of the month, when their pay is due, they run riot around the village, firing into the air and shouting.

People here are very poor. Most go barefoot, their clothes falling from their bodies. Many people, their homes destroyed by the bombing, live in makeshift shelters and abandoned buildings. Children are rare, except in the hospital, where some are being treated for severe malnutrition. Those who could get their children to safety—to Brazzaville, for instance—have already done so.

I speak to Valentine, a young, local nurse who now works for MSF. Her story is typical: trapped in Kinkala when war broke out, she was separated from her husband and children, unable to get home. As the attacks escalated from military and rebels alike, she fled into the forest, along with much of the rest of the population. There they hid, without supplies, health care, or proper food, until the arrival of MSF—the first NGO to enter the area—in April. After that, people began to return. Her own children are safe with relatives in Brazzaville, and although the worst of the crisis is over she and the other medics are still dealing with the many casualties: war injuries, malaria, malnutrition, victims of violence and rape. There are still people in desperate need of help who simply can't get to the hospital. Supplies are low, even basics like suturing thread and paracetamol. Often, the medics have to improvise; every trip along that nightmarish road is another risk.

The next morning we accompany the team to Kibouendé, a rebel village some two-hour's drive from Kinkala, where a mobile clinic is held every two weeks to cater for those who are unable to face the long walk to the hospital.

There is already a queue in front of the clinic, a roofless building over which the aides have stretched a tarpaulin to shelter the patients—many of whom have babies—from the brutal heat. Nicole, who is in charge of operations here, has arranged a meeting with one of the Ninja chiefs, Pasteur Oyena, to try to gain access deeper into their territory. It is a delicate piece of negotiation, and she is not sure how such a request will be received, although the Ninjas have also benefited from MSF's medical aid and should in theory be amenable.

The Ninjas belong to a kind of Messianic religious group, led by their spiritual leader, Pasteur Ntoumi, who looks like a bishop in his long, purple robes—a bishop with dreadlocks and a big machine gun. There are three other men with him, and a heavily armed bodyguard in reflector sunglasses who looks about sixteen. In deference to the "no guns, no uniforms" rule, they meet outside the clinic. The rest of us stay tactfully out of earshot, although I would love to hear what they are saying.

131

Our presence here attracts attention; people crowd around. Everyone has a story to tell; everyone wants to be photographed. I wasn't expecting this—that these people want to be heard. They are hungry, impatient; their villages have been destroyed. The peace agreement has been signed; the Ninjas have honored their side of it. But what of the president? What of his part in the bargain? Where are the supplies he promised, the food, the repairs to the roads? The rainy season is beginning; soon it will be too late to make repairs. The road, already hazardous, will be virtually impassable for the next six months. They believe the president is making empty promises, trying to starve them out of their stronghold. They are deeply suspicious of his motives. If you were a rebel leader, hiding in the woods, with armed soldiers on three sides—you tell me—would you come out?

Perhaps they have a point. But I can't help thinking of some of the stories I heard from their victims: the rapes, murders, looting, indiscriminate brutality. Mahon-Djedra looks at me. Terrible things happened, he says quietly. It is his only comment.

What about the future? He shrugs. We don't want another war. We were civilians once; some of these soldiers are our brothers, our sons. We want to return to our old lives. But as long as Pasteur Ntoumi stays in hiding, we will not disarm. And if the president starts a war, we will not turn away.

That night we hear gunfire. Soldiers, says Nicole. A brawl. Who knows? We set off late, back to Brazzaville. It is busy; several times we are held up by broken-down lorries, and the heat is intense. After Kibouendé, however, we are no longer as nervous at the sight of purple scarves and machine guns; there are many roadblocks, but no one takes them really seriously. Three little boys try to hold us up, using a piece of bamboo and an upside-down American flag; on this road, it seems, everyone wants to be a bandit.

But our relief is premature. Less than an hour from Brazzaville, we are stopped at a roadblock. Half a dozen or more sullen-looking teenagers slouch on machine guns and rifles. We are not afraid; we know the drill. But this time, there is no smile, no wave. The barrier remains closed; the mission order returned unopened. One of the youths pokes the end of his machine gun through the open window. There follows a brief exchange in Lingala. The shouting, the angry gestures are enough to tell me that it is not going well.

They want money. Patrice shakes his head. We're MSF. We never pay. It's the most important rule: create a precedent, and suddenly anything becomes possible. Another heated exchange in Lingala; again, Patrice refuses. It occurs to me how easily such a situation could turn. Adolescent boys are unpredictable enough; add six AK47s, some hash, and the complete absence of law and order, and the result is anyone's guess. My guess is that they probably won't shoot us. They want to. They really want to. But Patrice has called their bluff, and they let us pass. Later I learn that this road—National Highway Number One—has an alternative, more picturesque name. Locals call it the Corridor of Death.

I fly back to England tonight, but it's hard to leave; it's as if something in this place has got into my blood. I want to know what happens next in Pool, in Voula, in Mossaka. Maybe this is why people risk their lives to work for MSF, to live on a tiny salary, in primitive conditions far from their families, all the while knowing that one individual can never, ever do enough, but doing it anyway, quietly, in hope.

How can a girl this young have
the look of someone so old?
When she arrived at the clinic
she was on the verge of death
with chronic malnourishment.
Now twice the weight she was
on arrival, she is almost strong
enough to go home.

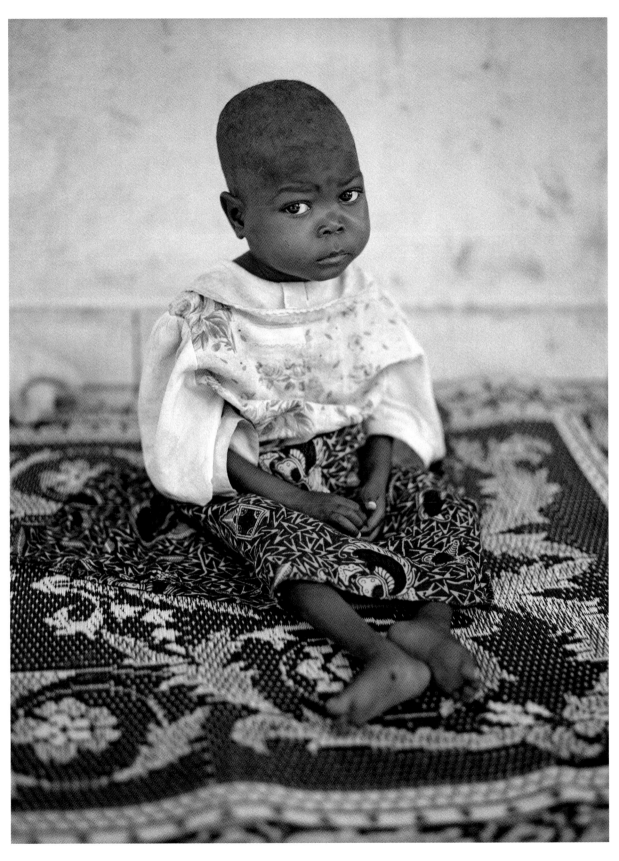

Without doubt one of the hairiest moments in the making of this book: standing on top of the most dangerous train in the world. The train runs from Brazzaville to the oil port of Pointe-Noire. It is an essential supply line for the capital city but runs through the heart of rebel-held territory, led by Pastor Ntoumi and his army, the "Ninjas." As I clambered on board the logging carriage to take a photo, I felt like the most exposed man in Africa, and as soon as I got down I was promptly arrested (the military commander who arrested me had his son saved by MSF and let me go).

A train station in the rebel-held Pool region between Brazzaville and Pointe-Noire.

Previous spread: MSF treats patients wherever it can. Here they wait patiently in a bombed-out building in the heart of the Pool region.

Morocco

The Pursuit of Happiness

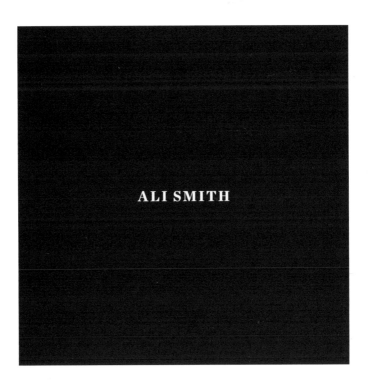

TAKE A FEW EVERYDAY WORDS, words we think we know the
meanings of, like tomorrow or doctor. Or trainers, ferry, fence,
or mobile. How about the words football stadium or network?
Or water bottle, or pregnant, or ladder, or view?

What about the word Europe? What does Europe actually
mean? How about a word like insight?

Insight

The English couple sitting next to me on the Casablanca plane have
got the word insight all over their hand luggage. Insight Vacations.
They're going to Casablanca first, then down to Marrakech, where
it should be a lot warmer than England in December. It takes less
than four hours to get from Heathrow to Casablanca, and for two
hours I've been having a jokey argument with the man about how
he's taking up all of our shared armrest. At the same time I'm
looking at the book of photos that Tom has brought to show me.

It's the work of a Dutch photographer who spent years traveling
around the world, taking pictures of the places where people with
no passports try to cross into other countries. There are pictures
from Morocco and Spain of people washed up on tough-looking
beaches, battered people huddled in blankets, bloated from being
in water too long, people dead on the shore. There's a picture
of a barbed-wire fence that looks like it's out of a sci-fi vision of
a totalitarian hell. There's hardly any text. What there is says
that in the year 2000, 15,000 immigrants were picked up on the
Andalucian coast trying to get into Spain from Morocco. It says that
along with the three-meter-high barbed wire, the infrared cameras,
and the searchlights, the officials in the town of Ceuta, the Spanish
enclave at the northern tip of Morocco, have put bars on all the
sewer outlets. It says that the identifiable bodies are returned home
at their family's cost, and that there's a cemetery in Algeciras full
of stones marked with just the letter D for desconoscido. Unknown.

We are traveling to Morocco to visit the MSF team working with
illegal sub-Saharan immigrants in the north. Because of a recent
tightening of measures against illegal immigrants, it's currently a
small but very vulnerable group. This vulnerability was evident in
October 2005, when the Moroccan authorities rounded up 1,200
immigrants—many pregnant women and people with TB, people
too ill to be summarily dropped back at the Algerian border as
usual (it's against Moroccan law to expel or deny treatment to a sick
or pregnant person)—and dumped them in a no-man's-land below
Bouarfa, in the desert, miles from anywhere, with no food, water,
or shelter.

Our plane food arrives. The man from Insight Vacations jogs
my arm for more room.

Ladder

In the MSF office in Rabat the notice board is covered with press cuttings from the Spanish newspapers about the immigrant situation. In all the portraits the faces are blurred. Javier, the head of the mission, explains to us that it might be difficult to photograph people since those filmed by the international media recently were caught and jailed.

The first illegal sub-Saharan immigrant we meet has a face that's all gentleness. He is an extraordinary man. When we ask him what he'd like to be called in this article he suggests the name Pascal. He's an unofficial liaison for MSF with the immigrant communities in Rabat; before he came to the city he'd been a translator. Pascal is witty and wry; he laughs a lot, a low and thoughtful laugh. One half of an index finger is gone from one hand. He is thirty-six and clearly brilliant—a microbiologist originally from Cameroon, which he left in 2003 because of a "family problem, a social problem" about which he looks panicked. He won't elaborate. "Right now I want to go back. If I go back my life will be in danger."

Traveling without a passport, he hitched and trekked to the international migrant junction Agades in Niger. There was a lorry leaving that day for Libya. He spent two weeks as one of eighty people in the lorry in the desert. They had a little food and just enough water. He tells me about the men in a car with no water for over a week who survived by drinking their own urine. "The desert: the most beautiful place I have ever seen, and the most dangerous. We passed corpses."

It wasn't a dream of Europe for Pascal. "I had a job. I just wanted to go far from my country." But religious intolerance in Libya drove him to try for "Europe in Africa," as he calls the northern Spanish enclaves, and he trekked 130 kilometers in the dark, off-road, sleeping in the snow, to reach Gourougou, an immigrant camp outside Melilla. Five hundred people lived there in tents made from blankets and plastic supplied by MSF, living in separate national communities: Nigerian, Senegalese, Malian, fifty people from Cameroon. They were all keen to "jump the fence," which is only the start of dodging the police on the way to breaking into the designated Spanish refugee camp. If you get in (like some obscene version of a children's game of tag), you'll be given expulsion papers, which guarantee you'll be taken to the Spanish mainland. If they catch you outside, they eject you immediately. It's much harder than you'd think to become an accredited refugee.

"The first thing they say to you when you arrive is, can you make a ladder? Your passport is your ladder! The only thing you take with you into Europe is a ladder. You need two ladders. One for each side of the fence" He laughs, charmingly. "I made many ladders. I entered many times."

This slight man has done what in a week's time, when I've seen the fences and the patrols, I'll know is close to superhuman. He's broken in and been ejected, not just once, but six times, surviving finally in a quarry for an epic eleven days, fed on the quiet by the Algerian quarrymen, before giving himself up out of desperation.

After this Pascal trekked 437 kilometers to reach Ceuta and tried to swim around the notorious fence there, some of it underwater, only to be turned back twice.

Network

Javier Gabaldon, head of the MSF mission in Morocco, came here after a mission stint in Rwanda, at the time of the massacres. No wonder he's a sanguine man, with an air about him of both care and irony. "Immigration," he says, "is a long process with a long resolution. Every situation is different, every immigrant group is different, every individual profile is different."

What these all share in Morocco is a current vulnerability to institutional and mafia bullying. The immigrants have access to two "networks" for help: one is MSF itself, the only provider of immigrant statistics and immigrant aid in Morocco. The other is the sinister Nigerian Network, which has made a massive difference in the immigration situation here over the past two years. Human trafficking is big money. It costs between five thousand and eight thousand euros to get as far as Morocco. "You pay the bill. High interest. Women will most often pay in sex work." MSF often ends up looking after people abandoned by the Network.

At the moment though, most of the violence against immigrants comes from the impatient Moroccan security forces that seem convinced that systematic harassment is a useful force in dissuading immigration. In summer 2005 all the inhabitants of a forest camp in Bel Younech in the north mass-rushed the security fence in an "organized" rebellion to try to enter Ceuta. No one succeeded. Fifteen people died of injuries sustained after the security forces shot and beat them.

It's possible to see the "mistake," as the security forces call it, of dumping the 1,200 people in the desert, as a bit of institutional vengeance in the wake of this. Right now Javier is handling the damaging aftermath of media excitement about it all, which a couple of international news networks have overblown into a "genocide" that caused more local and government anger and resentment at the immigrant situation. Javier is angry too. "It isn't a genocide," he says, "and to call it what it's not endangers what we are doing. What we are doing is basic and essential. There is no one else here to provide shelter, food, or somewhere to get clean."

MSF has worked with respect, gently, and firmly to insist on the authorities' responsibilities. Five years of a strong mother-and-child program has helped gain respect from and put pressure on the complicatedly bureaucratic and hierarchical Moroccan government system. "We want change to happen. It's not for publicity," Javier says. "It's for change." One way of keeping pressure focused, though, has been the publication, late last year, of the Moroccan MSF team's persuasive Violence and Immigration Report.

Here are a few of its facts. Migration is rising unstoppably. In twenty-four months MSF has attended to 9,350 medical consultations in Morocco, and an alarming number of these were due to violence against the immigrants. About 10 percent is Network violence, but an appalling 67 percent is from the actions of the Spanish and Moroccan security forces, with the Moroccan forces answerable for 52 percent.

Right now the majority of immigrants in Morocco—about two thousand—are almost totally abandoned, with no way out and no way home. Morocco has stopped repatriating; the remaining groups are those without embassies who'll take responsibility for them. Most of them are living in the poor neighborhoods of this rich city.

Pascal takes us to an undercover house where I meet a twenty-six-year-old man, B., who is sitting on a mattress. Next to him is a pair of prosthetic legs, almost like another person in the room. B. is befuddled and damaged, full of dignity and hurt. He was an electrical worker trying to get to Europe to make money to send home. He can't remember his time crossing the desert, because in February, when he was running away from the police who were stoning him, he fell under a moving train and mangled both legs below the knees. He's been here eighteen months.

The house is full of people, several sleeping in each windowless room. On the top floor, two girls, aged five and three, run about delightedly. One runs toward me and gives me a big hug, until she realizes I'm a stranger and backs off. Their mother is suspicious but agrees to talk to me. She came here "on a flight" (via the Network?) from "the Ivory Coast." She was a business traveler in France and Italy, in leather goods. But her business went bust (the war, and so on). She "knew someone" in Rabat, so she came here. Now there is nowhere for her to go.

It dawns on me that most people are lying when they tell you their stories. The discrepancy between their stories and their truths is clear. The stories they do give are given guardedly, pared down, full of the unsayable. Two things stay with me from this visit: the passionate articulacy of a man of about nineteen, who says to me directly, "there is nowhere to go from here. Please tell people. It is very important. It is not human." And the room the children live in with their mother, nothing in it but a mattress and an array of bottles of cheap moisturizer, baby oil, and cleaning products, lined up precisely, tallest to smallest, in the corner like a neat shop, with newspaper pictures of blonde models and film stars stuck above this on the wall.

All the way back to the rich part of town I wonder about a woman who refused to be interviewed by me, about whom Javier told us. She was raped twice in the same month, once by the security forces, once by the Network traffickers. Now she's pregnant and HIV-positive, still with her husband, with whom she traveled from the Congo. Abortion is illegal in Morocco. "Who will help her?" Javier said. "What can we do to help her?"

Ferry
Rabat is the European capital of Morocco, with its neat municipal streets, coiffured trees, Snoopyburger outlets, Ikea-like shops, McDonalds McArabia burgers, and much-less-gendered cultural mores (I saw more women walking freely and confidently about the streets in one night in Rabat than I did elsewhere during my whole time in Morocco). But Tangier is a city on the edge, a city in economic metamorphosis, aspiring to a Europe so physically visible from its port that you feel you could literally reach out across the tiny bay between you and Spain and touch it. It is so close that my mobile phone switches effortlessly into Vodafone Espagne on some parts of the coast. This strait, between the tips of Africa and Europe, is the petrol route and has always been a highly contested business route. You can see Spain from every rooftop in Tangier, and Gibraltar from a few miles north. Farther along the coast, Spain is so close that you can actually see the propellers turning on the Spanish wind masts.

Tangier's waterfront is alive with spanking-new apartment buildings. Its cracked and pungent medina looks onto a busy working port that the Tangier authorities are hoping to turn into a tourist haven, making it a new center for tourism and retirement as soon as they finish installing the brand-new industrial and military port ten miles to the north. The police presence is strong. (On our second day there Tom gets taken in for questioning simply for taking photos at the port.) Tangier's Wali, or governer, is keen to "clean up" the city. He is planting, in new traffic islands all along the waterfront, "a flower for every inhabitant of Tangier"— not including the illegal sub-Saharans, obviously. By chance, on our way in the MSF van to return to the closest bush camp some immigrants who'd attended the weekly clinic—one listless woman with TB ganglia, one cheerful man with a splinted broken arm— we actually pass the Wali himself, in his designer suit, out in a convoy of about thirty like-suited men, marching up the central reservation on a photo opportunity, checking the new soil beds.

Doctor

Jorge, the doctor, holds a Tangier clinic once a week and spends the other days in the bush with Siham or Fed, seeking out the most vulnerable people. He is young, dapper, a man of combined calm and energy, firm and kind in every engagement with the immigrants who come to the clinic, who are almost all Nigerian (as are most immigrants currently in Tangier), in their twenties, and all of whom eye me, a stranger in their safe place, with severe suspicion. All the women are pregnant or carrying tiny children in their arms. Almost all the patients refuse to be photographed. Jorge makes them laugh, puts them at ease within seconds.

"Without trust," he tells me, "nothing would be possible. Without regular consultation, nothing. Without the phone link to the bush"—he holds up his tiny mobile—"nothing."

I sit in on the clinic in the small and spartan consultation room. E. is twenty-six, says he's from Liberia. He's been in Morocco for over a year. In October he jumped out of the upper window of a house the police were raiding and badly broke his ankle (the other man who jumped fractured his skull and died). The police left him on the road. He didn't call MSF for two weeks, by which time his leg was festering. Why not? I ask Jorge later. "He thought it might be his night for crossing to Spain," he says. "Then the next night, it might again. If he was in the hospital, he'd miss his chance." He explains to me about the mindset almost all of the immigrants have. "What's happening today doesn't matter because tonight I'll be on a boat and tomorrow I'll be in Spain."

Why do you want to go to Europe? I ask E. "People have more feeling there," he says. Jorge cleans his wound, tells him he'll have to go to Casablanca for further treatment, calls in the next patient. V. is twenty-six, listless, with no appetite. He is in a state of anxiety. He's lost weight. He thinks he may have a blood infection. He casts an uneasy look at me, then tells Jorge that he's impotent. Jorge checks him out, tells him it's not surprising he's tired, living the life he's living, assures him it's normal. He gives him a great deal of reassurance, and a course of vitamins.

Why do you want to go to Europe? I ask. "For a better life," he says.

C., a heavily pregnant twenty-four-year-old woman, comes in. She sits down. She is apparently having blackouts. Jorge tells her she'll give birth in about a week. "And when the waters break you have to phone me and I'll take you to the hospital," he says. "Why have you lost so much weight, why do you look so tired?" She is still cooking and washing for five other people in a house. "The men don't do anything." Jorge tells her to stand up slowly, gives her some medicine, takes out his mobile, asks her what her boyfriend's name is and what his number is. "I'm going to call him and tell him you have to rest."

Her sullen, sad face breaks into beautiful smiles when I ask why she wants to go to Europe. "I want to go to Europe," she says. "I need to go to Europe. I want to go to Italy. I want to go to Venice"

After she's gone Jorge tells me that the same "Spain tonight" mentality means that many pregnant women among the immigrants think tomorrow they'll be somewhere they can abort more safely than in Morocco, and then, when it's too late, they buy a drug called Citotec, or Misaproctol, smuggled in on the black market from Europe. It's an anti-inflammatory, one of the nasty side effects of which is abortion.

A woman comes in, also heavily pregnant. She says her periods have stopped now for five months. She opens her coat and a lot of cladding, jumpers, and cloth fall out. She's not pregnant at all. "If the police think I am pregnant, they turn a blind eye," she says. Jorge takes a urine sample, gives her vitamins, reminds her about the family planning dates.

The clinic supplies all its patients with sex education and a strong family-planning regime (which in itself puts pressure on the Moroccan government to supply the same for Moroccans in a country where there's next to none; MSF works with the health authorities in Morocco to put pressure on the government to provide this and HIV treatment).

Jorge studied in Seville, Madrid, and Liverpool (tropical medicine) and did his first six months with MSF in the Congo. He's been here nearly a year. He is joining an AIDS program next, somewhere else in Africa. Why choose this life, I say, when you could be comfortable with your own GP surgery at home, or work anywhere you like, with your qualifications, for big money? He smiles at me. "The best education in the field, and the fastest," he says. "There is no national affiliation, so nothing—no politics, no religious agenda—stops you from working to your best. There's a great deal of freedom in it."

We go to the bush clinics over the next few days, which means we drive out of town, then off road, up rubbly muddy roads, and we stop in the middle of nowhere. We get out of the MSF van. Within seconds what seemed a deserted landscape is teeming with people running out of the bushes toward the van. "Dr. Jorge!" people shout. "It's Dr. Jorge!" They cluster around him and Siham, the social worker; they slap him on the back, they hang lovingly on her arms.

Fence
"It is the Moroccan-Spanish border area where the majority of incidents occur," the Violence and Immigration report says on

page 15. That afternoon, Fed, the administrator, drives us to see the border. On the way he takes us past the impenetrable-looking forest where the largest camp was, before the rush on the wall and before the police slashed the plastic tents, burned the blankets, bullied the immigrants, and confiscated all the mobiles they could find. One thousand people lived here in what was pretty much a township with its own restaurant, law system, and 4 p.m. daily football matches in its own "stadium." Now it's a wreck of broken rubbish, but still the only shelter for a couple hundred people who spend their day out of the way of the security patrols, up in the cold crags of a nearby mountain they've named Tranquilos (peace), descending only at night. Last night the temperature was 3 degrees Celsius.

We arrive in a tiny village. But around a corner, the village simply disappears and there's nothing but fence, layers of fence, fences that rise up out of the sea to a full height of three meters, hairy with barbed wire. Between them, a heavily lit patrol road is manned by strolling armed guards. It's easily one of the most obscene things I've ever seen.

We go down to the ashy beach just to try to get a closer look at it. Out of nowhere we're surrounded by police and soldiers, armed, coming at us from all angles. A smiling moustached soldier shakes his head at us. Don't we know? We're not allowed to photograph the fence, or look more closely at it, without written permission. "We have it to stop *les negres* from crossing." Polly from MSF press tells him we're writing an article about how Europe is so close to Morocco. "And yet so far," he says, finishing her sentence for her.

Fed drives us to another small town also split by the fence, and Tom and I try to get as close as we can to it by scrabbling about in some back gardens. It's now properly dark, and the fence is like a luminous scar right through the country. It's huge. Between us and the fence there's a massive concrete moat full of holes. We can't get closer to the moat than about a hundred meters for more layers of barbed wire. A patrol car goes past every twenty minutes.

We drive back to the forest, where Jorg and Fed are meeting some immigrants to pass on twenty-five blankets; the weather is getting worse. Right around the outskirts of the forest there's a brand-new gash in the ground, a deep new foundation about nine days old. It's where a new fence is clearly soon to be erected. Jorge and Fed dive over the top of its thirty-foot earth bank into the pitch dark and sprint into the forest—doctors without borders alright. They're meeting the immigrants at the football stadium, where they're going to treat some serious blister burns from an accident with boiling water.

After this we pick up a Malian boy of about eighteen, who has a suspected kidney infection, to take him back to town for treatment.

We find him at the designated meeting place: up the mountain road and next to the mobile phone mast. He is shaking with cold, and very, very hungry. He is polite; he smiles shyly as he gets into the van.

Trainers

The roughness of existence for immigrants has heightened as we've come closer and closer to the edge of Morocco. In Rabat things looked very rough. In Tangier they are near unbearable. One of the city's tightened measures against its immigrants was a new law that heavily fined landlords for allowing anybody to inhabit a building overnight without passport details. It is under quite a bit of protective security that we get taken, on my last day in Morocco, to see an illegal immigrant pension in the medina.

If the stench in the street is strong, then the stench in the totally dark stairway of the house is enough to make us gag. We go up three broken floors and emerge on the sunlit roof—from which, as usual, you can see Spain. Eight men live here, in three dark and damp rooms, with a camper stove. One man, small and neat, shows me photos kept in a plastic laundry bag on a hook in the wall of his wife and small baby, both deported. He shows me his baby's birth certificate, which is laminated and kept under his mattress. He puts it away. I watch him later, washing out some plastic water bottles until they're unbelievably white, putting them away, then meticulously cleaning out the urinal and the drain that they use as a toilet, with his bare hands.

A huge man with a leaking eye tells me he worked in Spain for two years, and two lawyers tried to win an appeal for him to stay, but he was deported in 2003. He's made his way back. He wants to get back in.

"But there is no way we can get in now," a man in a Dewar's whiskey sweatshirt says. "It's tight. There's no way. I want to work. There's no work in Nigeria. I know about textiles. I can tell you the whole process of your clothes. I want to work from January 1st to December 31st. I don't need Saturdays or Sundays off."

A dead-eyed young woman walks across the roof. She says nothing, disappears into the dark. The men ask us for money. "Tourists have taken our photos before. It's not fair not to help us." One shows us the holes in his trousers. Another shows us the place in his Bible where it says that St. Paul walked to Spain. "He did this, like us. It says here." In the back of the Bible someone has written in colored pencil, "Jesus loves Innocence."

The men light the black stairwell for us with the screens of their mobiles so we'll get safely back down to the street.

Mobile

That final afternoon, we visit a secret bush camp in the hills outside Tangier. We drive through streets full of billboard ads for mobile phone networks and relentless ads for ferries to Spain. La Mer. Votre Plus Belle Route. The two female patients in the van talk about Vodafone and God.

I remember once seeing an elderly author on *Question Time*, who said in rich, dismissive tones about the British underclass, "How can they be poor? They've all got color TVs and satellite dishes. That's not poor." I think about the story of the last police attack on a bush camp like this, when they arrested three people and confiscated thirty mobile phones and all the money they could find, and about the man with the splinted arm who told me in the van a couple of days ago that he'd been attacked and had his money stolen, but had been clever enough to jettison his phone first: "I knew where to find it later." Mobiles mean contact with home; they mean contact with the Network, with leadership, with other immigrants, and with MSF. The immigrants contact the office by letting the number ring once then waiting to be called back.

We take a mud path up through bushes and down through greenery, and the camp suddenly opens out of nowhere, so well is it camouflaged, the green and blue plastic in the green bushes under the blue sky. One hundred and fifty people live here in a spread of tiny makeshift tents, against a perfect view of the port and the sea, the coast of Europe, the endless taunt of the ferries. The camp is squalid, full of rats and ants, nothing but packed black mud paths between scrubland and tents. But put people in the middle of nowhere and they'll make a community. Wherever they are, people will make a home. Men playing drafts with water-bottle tops as pieces leap up to offer us a seat because Polly is heavily pregnant; the seat is the only one in the camp, a broken, white plastic sun-lounger. A girl of about seventeen wearing a Barbie necklace is sitting in the mud with a clean pan of rice on one side, cutting up a piece of cardboard to use for her hair relaxant. Welcome, she says, and smiles.

The word we hear most often is "welcome." We are welcomed, a little suspiciously, but warmly all the same, at the door of every tent. Take your shoes off. Come inside. Stay for dinner.

There are several children: a smiling four-year-old boy dancing about, a couple of eight-month-old babies on their mothers' backs who are charming and happy, and in one tent a brand-new baby, two weeks old. Its mother asked her boyfriend to phone MSF but he told her to wait until morning. The baby was born there in the bush.

Over the hill, Tom finds the remains of the last camp, wrecked by the police in one of their frequent raids.

"Bring a plane," one woman says to me, "and fly us out of here." She flaps her arms, then all the women around her break into hilarity. "A humanitarian lady came here," a man tells me, "and she had visas and she got people out. Can you do that?" "How far is Scotland by boat?" another man asks me. "Do they need mechanics there?"

The people in this camp go to sleep every night looking at the lights from Spain, and wake up every morning to the Spanish coast in front of them. They haven't got a hope, and yet they're as full of hope as the little notebooks most people keep in their wallets are full of the close-written names and phone numbers of every European person they've ever met, the numbers of people who might one day be of help to them.

View

Is immigration dying down now that security measures are tightening? I asked Siham, the social worker, on the first day in the clinic. "No," she said. "It is quiet now, but I sense it will only get bigger, and worse."

In the last ten years, 6,300 people have died on the Spanish and Moroccan coasts, although official figures say it's only 1,400.

When we get back to the hotel after visiting the camp I stand and look out over the waterfront at the evening view of old and new Tangier. It's warm in Tangier during the day if it's sunny, but notably chilly in the wind and at night. Its streets are full of Moroccan men coughing like old horses.

Soon I'll be home, where the Sunday supplements over the Christmas fortnight will be full of articles on Exotic Morocco, Moroccan Tiled Palaces, Moroccan Hiking Holidays, Morocco and the Pursuit of Happiness. Even Dick Whittington, the pantomime about making your fortune, which I go to see on Boxing Day, will have its second half set in Morocco, or, as it's otherwise known, Paradise.

Never mind the views of Spain. I finally realize it. My hotel room has a direct view of the place where the hidden bush camp is. Like every tourist who ever stood on this balcony, the whole time I've been here I've been looking straight at it and simply not seeing it. Insight vacations.

Illegal immigrants in Morocco are constantly on the lookout: for the authorities, for nightfall, for a chink in the fence, a ride on a boat, a place to crawl under a lorry to get on a ferry. But most of all they are looking out to Europe. From this secret illegal camp in the hills above Tangiers you can see Europe: so close and yet so very far.

An illegal camp of sub-Saharan immigrants in the hills above Tangiers. They help one another along one of the world's most treacherous journeys.

A secret camp in the hills above Tangiers, where MSF provided basic but essential medical care to sub-Saharan immigrants who had traveled thousands of miles to get within sight of Europe.

One of countless fences and
barriers in Northern Morocco
to prevent the passage of
refugees to Europe.

African refugees become trapped in these Northern Moroccan towns and cities. They are out of money, unable to go home, unable to go to Europe, and ostracized by the local communities that don't want them there, yet they still have basic medical needs for which MSF has opened clinics.

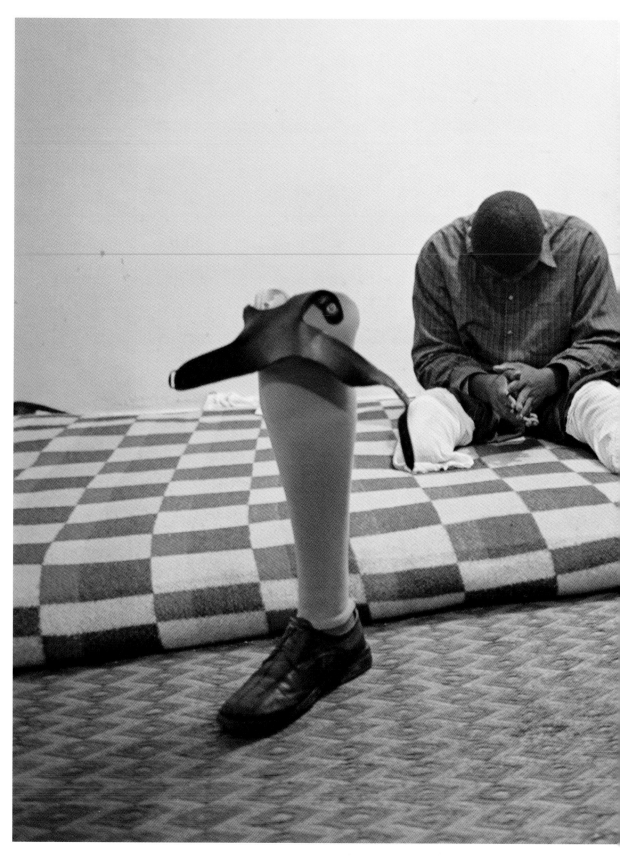

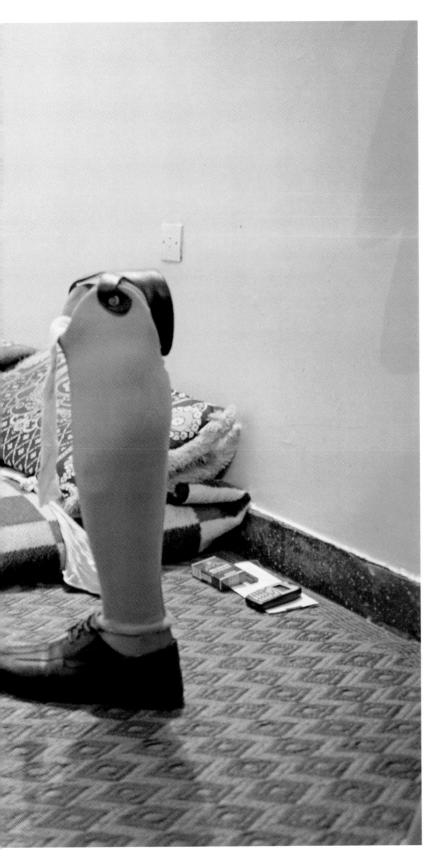

This man was on the run from the local authorities in Morocco, afraid that if he was caught he would be sent home. In the chase that ensued he fell beneath a moving train and lost his legs.

Illegal immigrants view anything as a mode of transport. This dilapidated fishing boat (left) or the ferry from Ceuta to Southern Spain (right) could offer that final hop to the place they dream of.

Palestine

How to Manage the Effects of a Military Attack

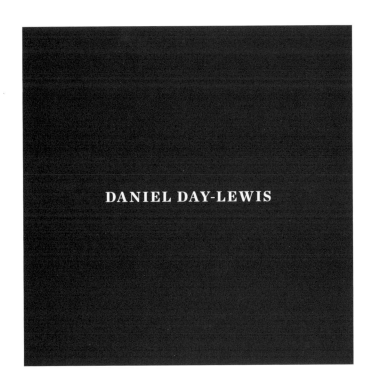

DANIEL DAY-LEWIS

TRANSCRIPT OF ISRAELI DEFENSE FORCES' radio communications: Gaza

Watchtower: "It's a little girl, she's running defensively eastward." (Away from army post and back toward the refugee camp.)

Operations room: "Are we talking about a girl under the age of ten?"

Watchtower: "A girl of about ten. She's behind the embankment, scared to death."

A few minutes later thirteen-year-old Iman Al-Hams was shot in the leg from one of the command posts.

Watchtower: "I think that one of the positions took her out."

At that moment the company commander, Captain R, left the post and moved toward the wounded and helpless girl. He shot her twice in the head, turned, and walked away. Then, turning back, emptied his entire magazine into her inert body.

Captain R: ". . . receive a situation report. We fired and killed her . . . I also confirmed the kill. Over."

Captain R: "This is commander. Anything that's mobile, that moves in the zone, even if it's a three-year-old, needs to be killed. Over."

Major Gen. Daz Harel, the officer responsible for the Gaza Strip, concluded that the Captain had "not acted unethically."

Abu Saguer has five sons and four daughters—"You'll go broke with more than that," he said. Initially it was the eldest, twenty-two-year-old daughter whom Sue Mitchell, an Australian psychologist on a six-month mission for Médecins Sans Frontières, was asked to treat. In Sue's experience the framework of each initial visit with a patient almost invariably expands to include other family members, friends, sometimes neighbors. No one is left untouched, and today, as we make our way across the broken ground, it is Abu Saguer's granddaughter Marvat whom Sue is visiting. Mossa'ab, our interpreter, leads us, carrying a white MSF flag. We are in full view of an Israeli command post now occupying the top floors of a five-story mill that is draped in camouflage netting—as is the house a short way from it. It is to this house that we are heading across two hundred yards of no-man's-land, the last one left standing in what had once had been an area teeming with life.

Civilians have been the main victims of the violence inflicted by both sides in the Middle East conflict. In the Gaza strip the Israeli army responds to stone throwing with bullets. In answer to suicide bombs and missile attacks on Israeli settlements it unleashes military ground assaults called "incursions." The bulldozing of houses and olive groves in search of Palestinian

168

militants and as punitive action against their families is just a part of such an operation. It also serves to establish "buffer zones" of uninhabited and uninhabitable land for the protection of Israeli settlements. The tanks and armor-plated bulldozers will come with no forewarning, often in the night. The noise alone, to a people who have been forced to suffer these violations year after year, is enough to freeze the soul. Snipers position themselves on rooftops. The occupants are ordered to leave—they haven't even the time to collect papers, clothes, or pans before the bulldozers crush the unprotected buildings like dinosaurs trampling on eggs, sometimes mashing one into another, then covering the remains with a scoop of earth. Those caught in the incursion zone will be fired on. Even those cowering inside their houses may be shot at or shelled through windows, walls, and roofs. Sometimes a family will not leave an area where the clearing is taking place, believing that if they leave they must surely lose everything. It is a huge risk to remain. Sometimes a house is left standing, singled out for occupation by Israeli troops. In these cases the family is forced to remain as protection for the soldiers.

This year an average of 120 houses were demolished per month, leaving 1,200 homeless each month. In the past four years 28,483 Gazans have been forcibly evicted by these demolitions, and more than half of Gaza's usable land, mainly comprising citrus fruit orchards, olive groves, and strawberry beds, has also been destroyed, drastically worsening a severe food shortage. Between January and September of 2004, more than 450 Palestinians have been killed as a result of the violence in Gaza, along with dozens of Israelis.

This plowing under, house by house, orchard by orchard, renders a community into wasteland, strewn and embedded with an obscene, stunted crop of broken masonry, glass, and toys, nails, books, abandoned possessions of all kinds. As we zigzag toward the house of Abu Saguer and his family we are treading upon ground replete with shattered histories and aspirations. Marvat is with us, a sweet, shy seven-year-old, with red metal-rimmed glasses, her hair in two neat braids held by flowery bands. She wears bright red trousers and a denim jacket. Last April her mother heard an Israeli jeep pull up and then drive off from the military access road in front of their house. Something, some projectile, had been fired, and when Marvat reappeared—she had been playing outside—she was crying and her face was covered in blood. They washed her. Her right eye was crushed. One month later an artificial eye was fitted. A special recommendation was then needed from the Palestinian Ministry of Health to finance a trip to Egypt, as the first eye was very uncomfortable. Now the Ministry has to negotiate each time for permission from the Israeli government to cross the border into Egypt where, every six months, Marvat has to have her eye changed. Fifty cars are permitted to cross each day; each must carry seven people.

This is Abu Saguer's story: his house was first occupied during the Second Intifada. (He wants Tom, who is covering this expedition, to take his picture and put it on every wall in England, Germany, and Russia.) He is fifty-nine years old. At the age of twelve he went to work, and at the age of sixteen he started to build the house he had dreamed of "slowly, slowly," as a home and gathering place for his extended family. He grew up in a house made of mud in Khan Unis, which let the water in whenever it rained, and all his pride and hope and generosity of spirit had invested itself in this ambition. He had worked in Israel, like so many here, before the borders were closed to all men between the ages of sixteen and thirty-five. (Unemployment in Gaza is approaching 70 percent.) For more than twenty years, Abu Saguer had his own business, selling and transporting bamboo furniture. During the second Gulf War, soldiers had stolen all his merchandise, and he relied, after that, on his truck for income. He had cultivated three hundred square meters of olive trees, guavas, lemons, palms, and pomegranates in the fields surrounding his new home. These were all uprooted, destroyed with no explanation, for no reason, by the IDF. For "security." Since that time a road that services the Israeli settlement of Gush Katif has been built, and during our visit the traffic passes freely, backward and forward, along the edge of that barren land where his orchards had been.

On October 15, 2000, Abu Saguer was with his wife in the house when the settlers emerged on a shooting spree. He and his family fled to Khan Unis. After four days he returned. He was hungry. There was no bread, no flour. He killed four pigeons and prepared a fire on which to grill them. The soldiers arrived suddenly, about twenty of them, and entered the house. He followed them upstairs. He asked, "Where are you going?" One took him by the neck and smashed his head into a door, breaking his nose. They kicked him down the stairs and out of his house. They kicked half the teeth out of his head and left him with permanent damage to his spine. "If you open your mouth we will shoot you." They left, returning in a bigger group one hour later, and occupied the top of his house, sealing the stairway with a metal door and razor wire.

The family lives in constant fear. The soldiers piss and shit in empty Coke bottles and sandbags, which they hurl into his little courtyard. They menace his children with their weapons. After two years of this the officer asks:

"Why are you still here?"

"It's my house."

Every bag of flour for Abu Saguer's household has to be divided in three and carried across the two hundred yards of wasteland. Everything must be carried. We are smoking apple-flavored shisha in the courtyard after a lunch his wife made of bread, tomatoes, olive oil, olives, and yogurt, all from the small plot left to him. "Take some puffs so you can write," he says. He speaks with great urgency, and my pen lags behind. Twenty days ago, a three-tiered perimeter of razor wire was laid to encircle his house. It was November 7, the beginning of Ramadan's month of fasting. This now forced him and his family to use the military access road, walking his children past tanks to get to school. It's a much longer and more dangerous route. There were ten tanks on one occasion, and after a week of this he was shot at from the watchtower. Abu Saguer gathered his wife and children, consulted with them, and then they sat down in the road. From midday until four o'clock they sat.

"If they crush us here I want a solution."

Jeeps passed by, nothing happened. At dusk they went in to break their fast. The next day a high-ranking officer approached them in the road.

"What's the problem? Are you on strike? What is it, are you upset?"

"Yes."

"A lot?"

"A lot, a lot, a lot."

"Are you upset with us?"

"I'm upset with the whole lot of you."

"Why?"

"You're forcing my wife and children to walk in front of tanks and bulldozers. I want a donkey and cart."

"Big donkey or small donkey?"

"Big, to pull a cart."

"Impossible."

(Abu Saguer, smoke streaming from his nose and mouth, says: "If they'd said yes I'd have bought a very big donkey to bite his nose, and donkeys that bite are very inexpensive.")

"Give me a gate then."

"We don't have gates."

"I'll make one."

He made a small gate from two pieces of wood and a wire grill. They asked him to buy a padlock. He bought one. A soldier accompanied him and supervised as he cut through the bottom tiers of razor wire (they wouldn't allow the top one to be cut) and installed his little gate. "If the gate is left open and anything happens we will shoot you."

Sue asks: "What's it like for you to tell this story?"

Abu Saguer: "I release what I have in my chest. I can't sleep. I woke this night at 1 a.m. I thought it was sunrise. I woke all the kids and told them to go to school. I look around and see that my life has been ruined. I'm like a dry branch in the desert."

Sue has a wonderfully calm and gentle presence. She quietly guides her patients to and fro, between the pain of their memories and a recognition and acknowledgment of their strength, courage, dignity, generosity, and astonishing good humor in the face of this desperation. Abu Saguer is a man of great affability, and because of his resilience, his wit, the tenderness he shows to the children, it's easy to think of his survival in heroic terms, but often he has periods of deep depression, disorientation, and forgetfulness. "I'm not scared anymore, I can't explain it. I just don't care. There's one God, I'll die only one time."

The soldiers have left but may come back. The family, however, does not go upstairs.

We walk through those rooms that were occupied by the soldiers. Curtains chosen with care by his wife a long time ago billow inward in unsettling contrast to the camouflage netting that hangs in front of the window. Abu Saguer's gate is visible from here. I imagine him approaching it across the broken ground, struggling with a bag of flour, and stooping to unlock and open that little gate.

For four years he has been afraid to leave his house, afraid to leave his wife and children alone. He is a prisoner, just as all Palestinians are prisoners within the borders of their country. The transparent facade of self-government is an absurdity. The Gaza Strip is a massive internment camp, the borders of which shrink as more and more demolition takes place, and within which the population rises, as it does in the Middle East, faster than anywhere else in the world. The entire Palestinian population of 1.4 million is being brutally controlled for the benefit of approximately seven thousand settlers living in oases of privileged segregation. It's taken me less than a week to lose impartiality. In doing so I may as well be slinging stones at tanks. As MSF France's president Jean Herve Bradol has said: "The invitation to join one side or the other is accompanied by an obligation to collude with criminal forms of violence."

As we leave Sue makes a call to base. Each movement must be registered with and approved by the Israeli District Civil Liaison (DCL). We hear that a doctor has been shot dead while treating a wounded boy at a crossroads in Rafah, which we had passed the day before.

The recently deceased Lieutenant General Rafael Eitan, chief of staff of the Israeli Defense Force (IDF) in 1982, once likened the Palestinian people to "drugged cockroaches scurrying in a bottle." In 1980 he told his officers, "We have to do everything to make them so miserable they will leave." (He opposed all attempts to afford them autonomy in the occupied territories.) Both the attitude and the policy seem to have been passed on and applied with great gusto. Every movement here in any of the so-called "sensitive areas"—borders, settlements, checkpoints, and so forth (which account for a large and ever-increasing proportion of the Strip)—is surveyed and reacted to from a system of watchtowers. These sinister structures cast the shadow of a malign authority across the land. Warning shots were fired at us twice, even though we were clearly identifiable as humanitarian workers. On our third day, standing at the tattered edge of the refugee camp at Rafah, the forbidding borderland between Gaza and Egypt, bullets ripped into the sand a yard and a half away from where we stood. Was it from the same watchtower that Iman Al-Hams, a defenseless thirteen-year-old schoolgirl, had been shot? Only weeks before my journey to Palestine, at home in the inviolate tranquility of rural Ireland, I had read the transcript of IDF radio communications that serves as a prologue to this piece. I had seen the photographs of that innocent girl's broken body and felt a pure dread of this place to which I was traveling.

Entering Gaza for the first time at the Irez checkpoint, we'd seen some Israeli kids in uniform. We'd seen them on the way from Jerusalem hitchhiking or slouching at bus stops, disheveled, sleepy, their uniforms styled and accessorized; shades, colored scarves; weapons slung across their backs. They looked like they should have been on their way to school. One girl soldier at Irez, wearing eye liner and lipstick, friendly, with the implied complicity of "we're on the same side," said: "I'm laughing all the time, I'm crazy." Most of them appeared indifferent, almost unseeing. We walked with our bags through the long, concrete tunnel that separates these two worlds. In the eyes of their bosses, we are a menace, Tom, Vikkie (from the London MSF office), and myself, because we're witnesses and, unlike the Palestinians, we can bring our stories back out of there. All humanitarian workers are witnesses. The United Nations is at present on phase 4 alert: the highest level of alert before pulling out altogether. They're a little tired of being shot at. Ambulances, hospitals, civilians—anyone might be fired on. There is no immunity.

We traveled south from Irez toward Beit Layia through the area "sterilized" during operation "Days of Penitence," a landmark Israeli incursion. There is not a building left standing that hasn't been acned by shells and bullets, many of them with gaping mouths ripped in them by the tanks. A vast area has been depopulated and ground into the rubble-strewn desert that we'll find wherever we go. A Bedouin encampment has settled impossibly on one of these wastelands. Half a dozen smug-faced camels and a white donkey stand behind the fence waiting for Christ-knows-what; the air is thick with the scent of them. The nomad families have constructed hovels out of sheet plastic, branches, and jagged pieces of rusting, corrugated iron. You could imagine these to be the last scavenging survivors of doomsday. Southwest toward Gaza City, the Mediterranean Sea appears before us like a mirage, shocking in its beauty: Gaza's western border.

We arrive at the MSF headquarters in the middle of the daily logistical meeting. Hiba, a French Algerian who will complete her eight-month mission in January, has perhaps the most stressful and complicated job of all: to organize and monitor throughout the day the movements of each of the three teams working here. She has to seek numerous "co-ordinations," which in the veiled dialect of occupation means permission to enter and leave any sensitive area of the territory. This she achieves, if possible, through an Israeli DCL area commander in the Department of Co-Ordination. We'd met one of them—just a kid like the others—at Irez. "Oh Hiba, she takes it all too personally," he'd said, as if the whole thing were a game, with no hard feelings, between consenting adults. Even with this "co-ordination," a team may arrive in the area to be refused by the local officer in charge (or in some cases to be shot at.) No reason need be given. "Security." An incident might occur at any moment that could alter the status and immediately affect the safety of the team. Hiba keeps in constant communication, assessing, reassessing, adapting. At any given moment the heavily fortified checkpoint at Abu Holi can be closed, effectively dividing Gaza into two parts, each inaccessible to the other. It may remain closed for four, six, ten hours. Yasser, the Bedouin driver of Sue's team, once waited for three days to cross. We had been held up there on one occasion. A babble of aggressive commands is continuously disgorged from the IDF bunker through new, burglarproof loudspeakers at the side of the road. Recently a gang of young boys had made a human pyramid and stolen the speakers. "Wah,WAh,WAH," the boxes yell at you from within their razor-wire cocoons. (Only taxis, trucks, and humanitarian vehicles are allowed to cross the checkpoint. No private cars.) At the end of each day, Hiba rests only when the teams are returned safely to their bases in the city of Gaza or in the southern region where another MSF apartment allows visits in that area to continue if the checkpoint is closed.

In the southern MSF base I'm awoken on our third day at 4:30 a.m. by the call to prayer—the mosques have loudspeakers too, and wherever you are you're never far from them—and then woken again at 7:00 by the surprising sound of children in a school playground. In any place, in any language, the sound is unmistakable. Gleeful and contentious. When you're in bed and you don't have to go to school yourself it's a delicious sound. Are they taught here, among other things, that they have no future? The windows from this side of the apartment all overlook a playground of pressed dirt with a black-and-white-striped goal of tubular metal at each end. The school, unmarked by bullet- or shellfire, is a long, two-storied building, constructed in an L along two sides of the pitch. It is painted cream and pistachio and resembles a motel in Arizona. (Later this day in the refugee camp at Rafah we'll drive past a schoolhouse riddled with bullet holes and meet a grinning ten-year-old boy, who proudly shows us the scar, front and back, where a bullet passed through his neck one day at school.) When classes begin, a teacher, in shirt, tie, and anorak, strides between classrooms, occasionally pulling a boy out to beat the back of his legs with a long cane. I move to the back of the flat where the kitchen is. From this window one sees, at the far side of a hand-tilled field warming itself in the early sunshine, two pristine houses, white and cream, like miniature palaces. The field is hemmed at one end by a row of olive trees and at the other by a large cactus. A middle-aged man and woman in traditional clothes move up the drills in perfect unison. The distance between them maintained, gestures identical, they advance, bent at the waist, planting one tiny onion at a time, plucked from a metal bowl. If an occupying force were ever in need of an image to advertise the benevolence of its authority, this would be it. I wonder what awaits these people, and I try but fail to imagine the roar of a diesel engine and the filth of its exhaust as a bulldozer turns this idyll to dust, erasing the scene as if it were never there.

Moving back to the other side now with a cup of cardamom-flavored coffee, I watch a fiercely contested soccer game in the schoolyard. Half of the kids have bare feet. There's a teacher on each side, in shirt and tie. One of them tries a volley, which, to shrieks of delight from both teams, sails over the wall behind the goal. Two seven- or eight-year-old boys with backpacks watch, their arms around each other. They turn and hug for a long time, then wander off arm in arm.

Sue arrives, and the co-ordination we awaited has come through. Having been shot at from the watchtower at Tuffah yesterday, we'd thought maybe they'd refuse it.

Yasmine is a grave, self-possessed nine-year-old (a friend of Iman's, the young girl murdered at the command post in Rafah.) She finally came out of her coma after a nine-hour operation to remove the nails embedded in her skull and brain. An exploding pin mortar had been fired into her house. Her father was hit in the stomach and can no longer work. I've held this type of nail in my hand. They are black, about 1½″ long, sharpened at one end, the tiny metal fins at the other presumably designed to make them spin and cause deeper penetration. We sifted through a pile of shrapnel at the hospital, all of it removed from victims. These jagged, twisted fragments, some of them larger than an iPod, were not intended to wound, but to eviscerate and dismember: to obliterate their victims. Yasmine lives close to Abu Saguer in a ramshackle enclave, the courtyard of which is shaded by fig trees. Across the "sterilized" zone that lies between them, she can see her cousin's house, but it remains inaccessible (the cousins are also Sue's patients). On the other side of a coil of razor wire, laid within feet of her house, runs a sunken laneway gouged out of the sand by tanks. When Sue first met her, Yasmine was terrorized, screaming and throwing up during the night. Bedwetting. These symptoms are very common. In areas such as this, leaving one's house day or night could risk death, and yet staying at home is no more secure. Nowhere is safe.

Yasmine, and countless other cousins, under the guidance of Sue, have prepared a show that, after many last-minute whispered reminders and much giggling, they perform for us. Yasmine is undoubtedly the force behind this. The power of self-expression is immense in her. As she recounts the story of her wounding, her voice rides out of her in wave upon wave of pleading and admonition. Her crescent eyes burn within a tight mask of suffering, her hands reach out to us, palms up, in supplication. At the end the tension in her fierce, lovely face resolves into the shy smile of a performer reinhabiting her frailer self when the possession has lifted.

Then there is a play, with sober, stylized choreography and a chorus of hand jives. In the third act a little girl, played by the four-year-old in the group, is shot by soldiers during a game of football. Her expression is deadpan, unchanging (she has witnessed much of the horror that's so far befallen her family, and she hasn't started talking yet). She lies obediently on the ground, splayed out and rigid. The mourners, curved in a semicircle around her, pretend to weep and wail, but they're all laughing behind their hands, and we laugh too. At the end they sing a song:

"Children of the world they laugh and smile, they go to sleep with music, they awake with music, we sleep with shooting and we wake with shooting.

"Despite them we will play, despite them we will play, despite them we will laugh, despite them we will sing songs of love."

Yasmine doesn't join the others as they cluster around us to say goodbye. Looking up, we see her leaning on the parapet of the roof, smiling down at us. Silent. Her dark face golden in the rich, syrupy light of dusk.

Sue will complete her mission of six months soon and will hand over her patients to the next team. Each psychologist treats about fifty families. The short-term therapy is invaluable but in some sense feels like a battlefield dressing with no possibility of evacuation for the wounded, nor the gentle environment that, with time, might have allowed them to heal. These stories are unexceptional. Every room in every humble, makeshift, bullet-ridden dwelling, in each of the labyrinthine streets of the camps, contains a story such as this—of loss and injury and terror. Of humiliation and despair. What separates Abu Saguer's and Yasmine's is that we carry those stories out with us. The others you'll never hear about.

Boys on a break from school in a yard that was demolished by Israeli incursions.

Previous spread, left: Jerusalem
Previous spread, right: A mother and her children outside their home, peppered with Israeli anti-tank rounds.

You can't take a picture anywhere in Palestine without the children making victory signs. On one hand it feels deluded; on the other it is a sign of how deeply ingrained the determination to win is.

This building and the surrounding area were destroyed overnight by Israeli incursions into Gaza.

Palestine is made of arid rocks from the hills. The Palestinians build houses out of the rocks, the Israelis knock the houses down, and the Palestinian boys pick up the rocks and throw them back at the Israelis. Israel is made of rocks too.

Sierra Leone

Cutting and Tearing

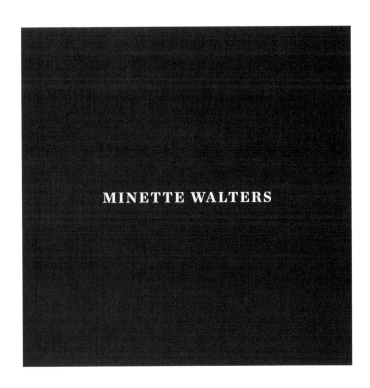

MINETTE WALTERS

IT'S ELEVEN O'CLOCK at night, and I'm in a medical operating theater in Kambia, a remote town in Sierra Leone. I'm using my weight to hold a pregnant seventeen-year-old girl to the table because there's no one else to do it. She lies in the crucifix position with each hand anchored to a wooden board, but her unfettered legs keep jerking and sliding toward the floor. A Dutch doctor and an Irish nurse are scrubbing up in another room, while two Leonean nurses hurriedly assemble the necessary anesthetic and equipment for an emergency C-section.

The closest I've been to childbirth was my own pleasantly painless labors, courtesy of epidurals, while my husband put on a brave face at the other end. I've never seen a delivery, except on television, and I've certainly never seen a cesarean . I try to look intelligent when Dr. Anne-Maria explains that the patient's suffering from eclampsia, but the only "eclampsia" I know is pre-eclampsia. Heads would roll in England if a consultant saw a seventeen-year-old in this state.

Her seizures have caused her to bite through her tongue, and it's so swollen that it's protruding from her mouth. To stop further damage, the nurses have jammed a stick between her teeth but, coupled with the crucifix position, it looks like a grotesque form of torture. Her name is Wara, and her husband brought her to the hospital half an hour ago. One of the nurses asked him why he waited so long but she knew the answer already. It took him twelve hours to borrow enough money to make the six-mile drive from their village. Sierra Leone is the third-poorest country in the world and, with no public transport, vehicle owners exploit the needy. The closer a patient is to death, the higher the price demanded.

Wara will die of system failure unless her baby is removed. The good news is the baby is still alive; Anne-Marie has picked up a heartbeat. The bad news is she knows nothing about this patient except that it's her first pregnancy. Wara's never been to a clinic, has never had her blood pressure checked or treated, and her husband's unsure when the seizures started because in this society men do not attend births. He can only repeat what Wara's traditional birth attendant (TBA) told him, and that information is unreliable.

TBAs have worked in Sierra Leone for centuries. They have herbs, containing active ingredients similar to Western medicines, which can stimulate contractions; but most of them use these herbs indiscriminately, without any real understanding of a mother's condition. The results of misuse can be horrific (excessive bleeding, ruptured placentas, retained placentas, obstructed labor, untreated eclampsia), which may explain why women in Sierra Leone have a one in fifty chance of dying every time they get pregnant, and why one in five of their babies is stillborn. As ten pregnancies per woman is common, death and childbirth are closely linked.

This operating theater bears no resemblance to anything I've seen on *Casualty*. It's a room in a house, and the table's so narrow that Wara's twitching body covers it entirely. I notice blocks of wood under the legs to raise it to working height, and I worry that each new convulsion will topple us over. Ancient wooden cupboards, stocked with swabs and sutures, stand in the corners, and dim light is provided by an outside generator. The two Leonean nurses work with their backs toward me, and I can't see what they're doing. There are shadows everywhere, and the smell from the latrines is so pervasive that I'm grateful for the surgical mask that filters some of the odor. I feel as if I'm in a Victorian novel.

Kambia Hospital was destroyed during Sierra Leone's eleven-year civil war. The war was declared over in 2002 after deployment of a large UN peacekeeping force and the deployment of British troops—a military intervention that, for the moment, Tony Blair can count as a success. The Revolutionary United Front surrendered its arms in exchange for money, and a desire for peace and reconciliation seems to pervade the country. Certainly, Leoneans are some of the friendliest people I've met in Africa.

With the hospital destroyed, MSF rented the largest available house and turned it into a sixty-eight-bed inpatients' department by building an extension and erecting a tent in the garden. There's no running water (medical staff scrub up under a tap connected to a plastic water container) and only intermittent electricity. Every bed is full, and each patient has one or more caretakers to cook and clean for them. Some days there are upwards of two hundred people milling around a house that was once used as a family home, and the heat can become unbearable. Even at eleven o'clock at night my gown is sticking to my back, and I wonder how Dr. Anne-Maria and Nurse Marion cope in the middle of the day, when the temperature outside exceeds thirty degrees Celsius.

In a country like Sierra Leone with high mother/baby mortality rates, specialist maternity care is essential. I'm shocked at how devastating full-blown eclampsia is and look up with relief when Anne-Marie and Marion return, fully gowned and gloved, to start the operation. I have no medical pretensions at all. I may write about murder but I'm not that keen on blood. I'm in Sierra Leone to observe MSF's Mother Child Health initiatives, not to participate in emergency C-sections.

With two professionals in charge, everything takes on a new urgency. A cordon of sterility is established, anesthetic's administered, and everyone starts barking instructions at me as if I'm part of the team. There's no one to direct the lamplight onto

Wara's abdomen so that Anne-Marie can see where to make her incisions. I'm ordered to the bottom of the table to hold it steady. I manage fairly well except for one small wobble when amniotic fluid suddenly sprays from Wara like a fountain. A few minutes later, Marion shouts for a fresh pack of swabs. I find them more by luck than judgment and succeed in opening the cellophane wrapper without contaminating the sterile contents because I'm too terrified to get it wrong.

Suddenly a tiny boy, weighing just over three pounds, emerges through the incision. He has virtually no color, he isn't crying or breathing, but he does have a heartbeat. One of the Leonean nurses scoops him into a green sheet and, together, she and Anne-Marie attempt to revive him with oxygen. We wait in silence until a thready cry and a sudden fluttering in his chest tells us he wants to live. It's an amazing moment that turns all too quickly to tragedy.

Marion, who's removing the placenta, has discovered another foot. This time it's a little girl, and she's half a pound lighter than her twin brother. Briefly, Anne-Marie tries to revive her but, with no heartbeat and only one oxygen set, she instructs all efforts to be concentrated on the viable baby. Later, I ask her what would have happened if the second baby had responded. "The same," she says with a sigh. "With only one oxygen set I have to choose the twin with the best chance of survival."

When I finally reach my bed an hour later, I fall asleep wondering if minor celebs who pay for "cosmetic" cesareans know how much cutting and tearing is needed to get inside a woman's uterus. If they do, they need their heads examined.

It's seven hours later. I'm in a 4 x 4, traveling north to Tombo Wallah with Isabel, a volunteer from Germany, and her Sierra Leonean colleague, Emmanuel. The thirty-mile journey to Tombo Wallah takes three hours: two hours on potholed dirt roads, then a further hour in a small wooden boat. Isabel and Emmanuel do these trips every day, and I admire their good humor and resilience. After bouncing around in the back of an MSF vehicle yesterday from Freetown to Kambia, my bottom feels shredded.

All MSF staff cite the difficulty of travel as a major cause of mother and infant mortality. Apart from the exploitative cost, the roads are so bad that only lorries and 4 x 4s can negotiate them successfully. In places, we see some road-flattening and hole-filling but new ruts open up as soon as the rains come. The only tarmacked roads in the north of the country were given and constructed by Germany in the 1970s and France in the early 1990s. I'm impressed by this sensible use of donor money in a country where corruption is rife. Finished roads don't disappear into government pockets.

Isabel and Emmanuel are MSF outreach nurses, and their job is to support the Ministry of Health primary-care clinics in the isolated communities around Kambia. Their focus is maternal and child health, and they train local teams to go around the villages with information on family planning, malaria, AIDS prevention, the importance of clinic visits during pregnancy, and safe delivery in the hospital.

Their target patients are women like Wara, whose tragedy could have been avoided with free antenatal care, but access to outlying communities is difficult and MSF workers believe they reach only a percentage of mothers at risk. That percentage keeps rising with 160 new consultations a month, but I hear numerous horror stories about what happens to women in the bush. Certainly Wara's experience suggests that if the drive to Kambia had been twice as long, she would never have reached the hospital. The life of a sick woman has less value than a man's, while the life of a sickly child has none.

The horror stories are too unpleasant to relate, but the difficulty of acquiring blood proves the point just as well. If a woman needs a transfusion in a country with no blood bank, someone in her family has to be persuaded to give a unit. It's a frustrating business. Relatives vanish mysteriously as soon as the request is made, and doctors waste precious time negotiating for the single pint that can save a wife or a daughter's life. By contrast, if an old man needs a transfusion, male volunteers queue for the privilege of helping him.

MSF's plan to support a state-run blood bank at Magburaka, four hours east of Kambia, has already run into problems. People are willing to sell their blood but they won't give it for free, any more than they'll give a free lift to a dying woman. Social responsibility is a Western concept that carries little weight in a country of subsistence farming, poverty, and malnutrition, where memories of a brutal machine-gun and machete civil war are still fresh in the minds. People smile all the time here, but I've no idea if they trust each other.

Rumor has it that Sierra Leone's palm-fringed beaches were once chosen as the setting for the Bounty "taste of the tropics" ads. They're certainly beautiful enough, as is the rest of this verdant sub-Saharan country. It should be land of plenty, but only a tiny percentage is cultivated. Skinny sheep and goats roam the villages, but it's rare to see pigs or cows. Tilling and planting are done by hand, and families grow only enough for themselves. Without roads and vehicles, their opportunity for trade is limited, and without money they can't buy seeds. In order to earn cash, they send their sons to Freetown or the diamond mines, and without sons to work the land, the land isn't worked.

It's a depressing cycle, reminiscent of England before the industrial revolution, and it can't be broken without huge investment in infrastructure. I ask our driver about Sierra Leone's diamond mines. Who owns them? Where does the money go? Like everyone else, he hints at corruption in high places and foreign businessmen with Swiss bank accounts. As this was the perception before the war, I wonder what all the death and destruction has achieved.

We approach Tombo Wallah by water, keeping a wary eye out for crocodiles. Wooden boats line its muddy, estuary beach, and tropical jungle sweeps the banks on either side. Single-story houses with rusted corrugated-iron or thatched-palm roofs border a yellow dirt road, and the vibrant mix of colors against a clear, blue sky is breathtaking. We wade through the shallow water, and children run to greet us with shouts of welcome. As we walk the two hundred yards to the clinic, they dance around us, clinging to our hands, and I understand why Isabel keeps volunteering for this kind of work.

The clinic serves a wide area, and there's a queue of patients waiting. Most can be treated by the MOH nurses who run the service, but serious cases are referred to Isabel and Emmanuel for possible admission to Kambia Hospital. Emmanuel takes the lead as he speaks Krio, a form of pidgin English that is understood by 95 percent of the population. Its alternative spelling is Creole, and it derives from the patois spoken by the liberated slaves who founded Freetown.

His first patient is Amie Turay. She's thirty-eight weeks pregnant and has been brought to the clinic by her elderly husband after complaining of pains in her abdomen. They've walked an hour to be here. She's an epileptic with a withered left hand and some paralysis of her left leg. She doesn't know how old she is but the nurses put her down as twenty-eight because her first child, a ten-year-old daughter, was abducted by rebels three years ago. As first pregnancies usually happen at fifteen, simple mathematics gives an approximate age.

To my eyes, she looks younger than twenty-eight, while her husband looks a great deal older, but impressions are deceptive in a country where the average life expectancy is thirty-seven. Amie is Mr. Turay's second wife, and this is her sixth pregnancy. She has two surviving children. Of the other three, the eldest was lost during the war, one was stillborn, and another died at two months old, probably of malaria.

Sierra Leone has the highest infant mortality rate in the world, with one in three children dying before their fifth birthdays. Malnutrition and respiratory diseases such as TB and pneumonia are common, but the major killer is malaria. In sub-Saharan Africa

2,800 toddlers die each day from the disease, and Sierra Leone, the worst affected, is still using chloroquine, a first-generation remedy that no longer works because malaria parasites have developed a resistance to it.

Lengthy discussions between the Ministry of Health, the World Health Organization, and MSF to persuade the government to adopt ACT (Artemisinin-based Combination Therapies) in place of chloroquine have finally reached agreement, although the government can't implement the change until the end of 2006. I hear rumors of a five-year stockpile of the old drugs that will retain their value as long as people believe they're effective, but I don't know if these rumors are true. In the meantime, MSF is ready to introduce the new drug into all of its clinics and hospitals as soon as it receives approval.

Mr. Turay agrees that Amie should return to Kambia with us, although he claims he won't be able to find a caretaker for her. I look at Amie and wonder what's frightening her. Does she think her husband will abandon her? I learn later that she's worried about the journey. She's never been farther than Tombo Wallah in her life and she doesn't know where Kambia is.

The next woman has edema (bloated legs and abdomen) and she's advised to come to the hospital as soon as she can arrange caretakers for herself and her five children. Her name's Asatu and she's very assertive. She tells Emmanuel that she doesn't like her husband, and she'll only admit herself to Kambia if the doctor will sterilize her without asking his permission. Otherwise she'll make a three-hour boat trip on the open sea and find someone in Freetown to do it. She's thirty-five years old, she's on her eighth pregnancy, and she doesn't want anymore children. With Emmanuel's reassurance, she agrees to come in on Saturday.

In countries where the next generation is needed to support a family, it isn't easy to persuade men of the advantages of family planning. With one in five babies stillborn and one in three dying in infancy, the law of averages suggests that there will be more living children if a wife gives birth every year, even though her own chances of survival diminish with each delivery. A man can marry again and father more babies to keep him in old age. A wife becomes redundant when childbearing is over.

Not unreasonably, women resort to subterfuge to protect themselves. They visit the clinics for secret three-month doses of an injectable contraceptive or, like Asatu, ask to have their tubes clipped during a cesarean. They blame their sudden infertility on illness or, if they dare, their hernia-prone husbands. A high proportion of Sierra Leonean men suffer from inguinal hernias, a bulge of intestine protruding into the scrotum. These are only dangerous when they're strangulated, so MSF's policy is not to operate unless the hernia is life-threatening.

Emmanuel is skeptical when a male patient claims his hernia of twenty years has suddenly become painful. The hospital would be swamped by men if he believed this story every time he heard it, forcing women and children to the back of the queue. He satisfies himself the intestine is sound and proceeds to manipulate it through the hole above the man's scrotum. I go outside rather than watch the poor fellow's agony. His testicle stretches to his knee and, though it seems a priority to me, it isn't. Hernias are unsightly but they don't kill.

I wander down to the riverside with a troop of children in tow, and find Mr. and Mrs. Turay waiting patiently in the shade of a tree. We can't communicate because they don't understand English, but as I hand out baby wipes to the youngsters, the couple draws close out of curiosity. I offer a wipe to each of them. Amie takes hers to clean her hands, and Mr. Turay tucks his surreptitiously into her bag so that she can use it later. I like him for that and hope it means he'll find a caretaker for her. When we finally board the boat, he stands in the shallows and waves goodbye until we're out of sight.

Amie looks so forlorn that I wish I could comfort her. It's lonely and stressful being with strangers, particularly if you don't understand what they're saying. When we climb into the 4 x 4 at the end of the boat trip, I ask Emmanuel to give her a sandwich, as I don't think she's eaten all day. "She'll be sick," he says matter-of-factly. "This is her first time in a car." But he gives her a sandwich anyway. I've never seen anyone eat anything so quickly, and I prepare to sacrifice my hat as a sick bag.

No one who travels in an MSF vehicle can be in any doubt of the charity's high standing. Everywhere we go, people wave and chant: "Em-ess-eff . . . em-ess-eff." I'm so accustomed to it that as we approach a village some half-hour from Kambia, I assume the people running toward us are being friendly until the driver slows to speak to them. One of their women is having problems with labor. Her name's Fatmata, she's thirty-four, and this is her sixth pregnancy. She's had one stillbirth, two sets of twins, and her TBA's worried that this labor isn't like the others. Isabel and Emmanuel decide to take her to the hospital.

The vehicle's already carrying eight passengers, and there's a whirl of activity as bags and boxes are tied to the roof in order to accommodate Fatmata and her caretaker. Amie has less idea than I what's going on (I learn the next day that she thought Fatmata's house was the hospital) but she squeezes up the seat and valiantly refrains from being sick. By contrast, Fatmata cries and clenches her fists all the way to Kambia, as every pothole we hit seems to encourage her to deliver. No one says anything. We're too busy praying that twins don't appear on the seat in front of us.

I spent a week in Sierra Leone, talking to patients at Kambia and Magburaka, where MSF provides free health care for mothers and children in a one-hundred-bed MOH hospital. Under the supervision of Sarah Bush, an MSF midwife from Sheffield, all staff are now trained to record patients' histories, with numbers of pregnancies, stillbirths, and infant deaths. The figures bear out the WHO and UN mortality statistics for Sierra Leone, although records only exist for patients who seek help. No one knows how many deaths go unreported.

While I was at Magburaka, there were six emergency C-sections in one twenty-four-hour period. This is not unusual. Women can be left to struggle for two or three days before they're brought to hospital, which is why MSF places so much emphasis on its outreach programs. Pregnant women in Britain take it for granted that their GP's surgery is their first port of call, but the concept of primary care for expectant mothers in Sierra Leone is a new one. When medical care had to be paid for, there was little incentive to take an apparently healthy woman for a checkup.

To reverse this perception, and teach prevention rather than cure, MSF provides its services free, relying on volunteer doctors and nurses from around the world to work six- or nine-month tours. Some, like Isabel, sign up again and again; others do single stints. I met a dozen different nationalities during my stay, and all were characterized by their professionalism and enthusiasm, and honest-to-God likeability. They're a rare breed, and it was a privilege to spend time with them.

Tragically, Wara's little son died after three days because he couldn't suck. His grandmother tried to keep him alive with milk from a spoon but, without specialist care in a premature baby unit, his chances were negligible. Wara recovered well from her surgery but it was a long time before her tongue healed. Her husband still has to repay the money he borrowed to get her to the hospital.

Mr. Turay surprised everyone by coming to Kambia himself to act as Amie's caretaker. Anne-Marie tells me he's looking after her well, and they seem happy together. I have a huge soft spot for Amie. Through a translator, I asked her the next day how she felt about her ride in the 4 x 4. She giggled. "I liked it," she told me. "It's the most exciting thing I've ever done."

Me too, I thought.

This village near Kambia was repeatedly destroyed during the eleven-year civil war. There was virtually nothing left: no electricity, no running water, and barely any housing. It was astonishing to see these women walking down the road on their way to a ceremony. To look so perfectly presented and beautiful under such difficult conditions seemed an incredible triumph.

Patients and family members
waiting outside the ward at
Kambia Hospital.

Fatmata was in labor when we found her at home while on MSF outreach. We all squeezed into the 4 x 4, and she screamed all the way to the hospital as we bumped along a nonexistent road. While she gave birth at the hospital, she didn't let go of my hand. This made taking pictures very difficult, but it was a magical moment.

A street scene in Kambia.

The road back to the bush.

Sudan-Nuba

The Geography of Hope

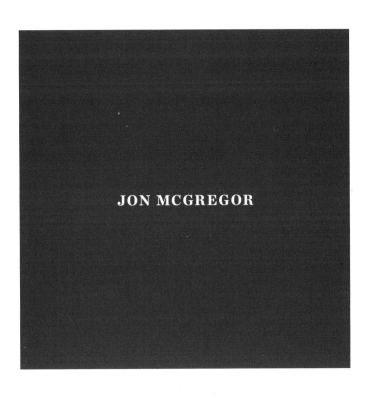

JON MCGREGOR

SUNDAY AFTERNOON at the Lemun Basic Healthcare Clinic, in the Nuba Mountains of Sudan, and a group of men is gathering beneath the shade of a baobab tree: a guard, a health worker, the fathers of children staying in the wards. They fetch picks and shovels from the guardhouse, waiting a moment to see if anyone will join them in their work. Their children sit quietly on rope beds in the shadowed mud-brick wards, or play outside in the softening afternoon light. Their mothers keep an eye on them, crouching by small cooking fires, talking, carrying plastic jerry cans of water back from the well on their heads, coaxing pale-haired babies to their breasts, watching the men from a distance. Chickens scratch around the sandy compound, looking for spilled scraps of food.

The men turn and walk out along a narrow path between fields of sorghum and maize, down to the stream. A woman washing her family's clothes glances up in greeting as the men cross over the stepping-stones. *Salam*, she murmurs. *Assalamualaikum*, they reply, *ahlamdulillah*. Following the line of the stream, wading through the long grasses still wet from yesterday's rain, the men walk quickly, silently, their tools slung over their shoulders. A boy herding his father's goats stops to watch the procession, staring, calling out to ask the men where they're going. *Kwes?*, he asks—how is it?—but gets no reply. Striding on, the men reach a low hillock at the far end of the valley and climb up to a patch of ground scraped clear of grass.

One of the men, Ismail, reaches the spot first and starts to dig. The others watch as he lifts the shovel over his head and brings it down hard into the stony ground, swinging it with something almost like fury, quickly working up a sweat as the damp soil sprays across his face and his green hospital scrubs. After a few minutes he straightens, rubbing his back, passing the shovel to another man, catching his breath. The others take turns to break up the solid ground, working in bare feet and broken sandals as the afternoon light colors with the expectation of thunder and rain.

Our journey through the Nuba Mountains began in Tangal, a well-populated village to the south, where MSF runs one of four health outreach units. As we walked from the airstrip to the clinic in the late afternoon we passed lines of people coming back from their fields and from the market, children bringing their goats in for the evening, old men standing and talking at the crossroads. But despite seeing so many people, and despite passing a school, a church, and a busy mill, we never arrived at a recognizable village; the small one-room houses were scattered across the valley and up the sides of the hill in groups of no more than two or three, their stone walls shielded by ripening sorghum stems. They looked like houses that were trying to hide. I asked Carbino, our translator, why the village was so spread out like this; perhaps it was traditional, I asked, or a result of the distribution of farmland? He thought for a moment and waved his hand at the sky.

"Yuh," he said, "actually, it's safer like this. This way, they are not a target."

A clustered group of houses is easier to see from the air, he explained, and to bomb. A traditional village, grouped around the well and the mill and the meeting square, can be surrounded, and when one roof is set alight the rest will quickly burn. The villagers of Tangal had scattered in the early days of the war, as villagers all over Nuba had done, hiding their homes high up in the hills, looking for a safety that wasn't always there, and they weren't yet ready to regroup and rebuild.

Not far from the compound we met a woman walking back from her field on crutches. Half of her left leg was missing, and after Carbino had greeted her and introduced us, he asked her our obvious questions. She paused a long time before answering, puckering her mouth around the words in distaste as if she'd eaten one of the locally grown sour oranges. "She says she walked on a mine," Carbino told us. "Over there, when she was tending her crops." He pointed to a field on the other side of the stream, five or ten minutes away. "She lost her husband and her children in the war. She is all on her own here," he said. She told him she was eighty years old, although she looked no more than forty-five. We asked, does her leg still hurt? And she turned away, shaking her head, as if the question was foolishness itself.

Sudan is a vast and complicated nation. Created almost as a cartographer's convenience from a shifting collection of tribal lands and alliances—Dinka, Nuer, Nuba, Arab, Fur—by the colonial powers of Egypt and Britain, Sudan has experienced peace for an all-too-brief eleven years since gaining independence in 1956. The most recent war, which started in 1983 and finally seems to have ground to a bloody halt—Darfur notwithstanding—can broadly be described as pitting the ruling Arabic and Islamic GoS (Government of Sudan) in the north against the predominantly Christian and black SPLA (Sudanese People's Liberation Army) in the south. It's been a war fought over land, resources, the right to self-determination, and the personal vengeances that gather their own malevolent momentum in any civil war. And oil, the poisonous treasure buried beneath so many of the world's conflicts, has had a role to play as well, particularly in the Nuba Mountains, which lie directly between the oil fields and the main export route of Port Sudan.

The war came to Nuba with a particularly relentless brutality, bringing suffering that has been described by African Rights as a policy of slow genocide. In an attempt to clear the Nuba Mountains of its population, the government forces destroyed food sources and infrastructure, carried out extra-judicial killings, and intimidated or forced villagers into specially established camps away from their own areas. The suffering of the Nuban people was heightened by being hidden from the world—outsiders were barred, and not even the UN's Operation Lifeline was allowed access to fulfill its mission of feeding the starving. It took a long time for the rumors of what was happening in Nuba to reach the outside world, and even longer for the suffering to come to an end.

The geography of the conflict in Nuba was complex, with frontlines shifting between the rainy season and the dry, with GoS garrisons planted like hostile outposts in the middle of SPLA territory, with houses and churches and mosques (Nuba, crucially, being both Christian and Muslim, refuting the simplistic claim that this has been an exclusively religious war) burned and rebuilt several times over the years. I lost track, as we walked from one clinic to another, of where exactly the front lines had been, whose territory we were on at any one time, why a particular mountain range had been such a vital battlefield. But one factor is key to understanding the war and the Nuban landscape. When the GoS attacks began—aerial bombardments, cattle raiding, kidnap and forcible relocation, the burning of homes and food stocks, summary executions, rape—the Nuban people, who have traditionally lived on the fertile plains and valley floors, ran for the hills and stayed there. Cut off from their homes and their farmland, they built new houses in small, isolated groups, carved steep terraces out of the rocky hillside, and searched, often fruitlessly, for adequate grazing for the few goats and cattle they had left. And now, with a two-year-old ceasefire and a peace process beginning to take hold, people have tentatively started moving down to the plains and valleys again, and coming back from their self-imposed exiles in Khartoum and elsewhere. They are returning to their old homes, rebuilding their villages, planting again the fields their families have worked for innumerable generations. The geography of the Nuba Mountains, I began to understand, can be read as a geography of hope, albeit a hope with deep scars of hardship and pain and irrevocable loss.

That first evening we heard what sounded like gunshots echoing down from the hills. But Carbino assured us that it was boys playing with sorghum sticks. "They heat them up in the fire," he said, "and then hit them against a rock—bang! It's the war-traumatized children," he added, casually, "they remember things, and they want to be soldiers."

After a few days in Tangal we walked out, following the route taken by patients who get referred from the basic outreach units to the better-equipped clinic at Lemun. The outreach units are able to deal with only the simplest of life-threatening diseases: the more easily diagnosed strains of malaria, the diarrhea and vomiting to which children are so fatally prone, chest infections, wounds. Anything more complicated—TB, other strains of malaria, malnutrition, anything that might warrant a blood test or admission to the wards—means that patients have to be referred to Lemun and make their own way there on foot.

I asked Carbino how far it was. "It's not far," he said, "I think maybe ten hours." He paused, looked at me again, and corrected himself. "Yuh, for you Jon?" he said, grinning, "I think two days."

They were two of the toughest days walking I've done in a long time. Striding out at a remorseless pace across dusty, shadeless plains, up steep mountainsides, down narrow paths treacherous with shale and loose rocks, I wondered how many people were unable to make the journey.

The clinic at Lemun is the nearest thing the area has to a hospital. There are no surgical facilities, but there are inpatient wards, a pharmacy, a laboratory, a therapeutic feeding center, and around eighty local staff members. Dozens of people arrive each day, waiting patiently on narrow benches beneath a brushwood shade, waiting for medicine, for treatment, waiting sometimes for miracles that can't be performed. Without a surgery, even appendicitis can be fatal here.

I accompanied Sook Lin Yap, one of the MSF nurses, on her morning tour of the wards. Each ward, a low mud-brick building with a grass roof and a packed-earth floor, has seven or eight beds squeezed into it, and we had to pick our way carefully between cooking pots and jugs of milk, ducking under mosquito nets strung from the roof like washing, as Lin introduced me to the first patient.

"This boy's two and a half; he's been here for six days," she said, taking the boy from his mother, asking her in Arabic if the child was eating well as she smiled and pulled faces, looking at his tongue and the whites of his eyes, feeling his skin. "When I first spoke to her she knew I was worried," she said, passing him back to his mother, "because I really thought I was going to lose him. But he's gained weight nicely, huh?"

She moved on to the next bed, crouching beside a pale three-year-old boy lying across his father's lap. "This child I was very concerned about," she said. "He had malaria and became very anemic, and what he needed was blood. But I haven't got it. So I put a tube down instead, and gave him good nutrition, and hopefully, you know, his body will make his own blood." Hopefully was a word I heard a lot from the international MSF staff in Nuba, a secular version of the Arabic *inshaallah*, God willing. Hopefully he'll pull through. Hopefully the family will give the medication properly. Hopefully the ceasefire will become permanent and the people here can start to rebuild their lives.

She worked her way around the ward, discharging a girl who'd had swollen knees, a girl with a chest infection, a boy who'd recovered from malnutrition. She showed another nurse a young boy with a kidney disorder, nephrotic syndrome, explaining how to look for the symptoms, explaining the limited treatment available. "Basically, we can give him steroids, we can give him drugs to make him pee," she murmured, "but this child won't get better, hmm?"

In the last bed in the ward, she came across a young mother with a very underweight-looking child. "This is Bethlehem!" she announced, recognizing the child who'd been carried in during a rainstorm a few days earlier. "And she gained a hundred grams, and she's eating and drinking well, and she looks happy, huh?" Bethlehem's mother, Nafisa, smiled at Lin's obvious delight. She looked a lot more relaxed than when she'd first arrived with her husband, Isaiah. Then, they'd watched helplessly as Lin and the others had gathered around the wailing Bethlehem, taking blood, preparing a tube, asking questions, both of them exhausted after walking for two days to bring their firstborn daughter to safety. Now, they shone with relief as Lin explained that she was ready for home food, and that they could feed her on demand until she was ready for the journey home.

I asked Lin about malnutrition, about its effects and its causes. She told me that very few children die of lack of food alone, that usually it's combined with something else: malaria, vomiting, diarrhea. Hygiene is often poor, she said, and the diet is already a limited one, lacking in fresh fruit or vegetables, lacking in meat or eggs, lacking in anything much beyond a thick, sweetened porridge made from sorghum. The treatment is simple though, she explained, if the parents are able to bring the children to the clinic in time. Rehydration and high-calorie food supplements combined with hygiene education are usually enough. When the children first arrive they are weighed—invariably bursting into tears as they're put into a bucket slung from a set of grocer's scales—and measured, and are then not discharged until they regain a height-to-weight ratio of at least 80 percent.

"Really they should be 100 percent," she said, "but no one's ever 100 percent around here. This child, Bethlehem, was 74 percent when she came in, and that's low, that's ill. I was surprised she could drink for herself. I've got a child in Ward 3 with a height-to-weight ratio of 57 percent, and if he makes it he'll only be my second one who made it from less than 60." She looked at the floor for a moment, faltering, and I remembered talking to her about why she was working in Lemun, asking what had brought her all the way from Malaysia via London to the scarred heart of Africa, and being struck by the simple sincerity of her response: that she loved having the opportunity to make a real difference to people's lives.

"He's only four years old, and he's in a bad way though, huh?" she said, about the boy in Ward 3, Mustafa Phillis. "Mostly, when they're that low, it's too late. Their bodily systems have been too badly damaged." Do many children die here? I asked. "Yes," she said, lowering her eyes again. "Lots do, especially now, during the malaria season. But this child will make it," she added, brightening, smoothing down the brittle hair on Bethlehem's head. "I can guarantee that, 100 percent."

Nafisa and Isaiah sat on the narrow bed with their baby, looking up at the two of us, wondering what we were saying.

Mustafa Phillis died three days later, in the early afternoon. It's his grave the men are digging now, barely an hour after his death, out at the far end of the valley with the other small and freshly dug graves. There are eight others where they're digging, low graveled mounds ringed with rocks. These are only from this month, one of the men says, the rest are there, and he gestures up and over the low hillock to where the long, wet grass hides numerous other small and unmarked mounds of earth. The men dig, and rest, and glance anxiously at the darkening sky. Ismail has brought a short stick with him, to measure the length of the hole they must dig, and he lays it out along the ground occasionally, muttering instructions to whomever is wielding a pick at the time. The man in the pale brown kurta, the father of the boy with nephrotic syndrome, kneels in the hole and scoops out loose soil in his clenched fists. Four of the other men return from the hillside with large slabs of stone on their shoulders, heavy graveside rocks that necessarily make them move with a funereal swagger. Another man fetches a jerry can of water from the stream. Thunder crackles in the near distance, storms pouring down onto other valleys.

Carrying rocks, in this heavily gendered society, is something men do, for building materials, or for land clearance. Men build and rebuild houses, work the land, dig the graves, and fight the wars. Women carry water, collect firewood, cook, bear children, and lead the mourning at funerals. But Mustafa Phillis's mother will have to wait until she gets home before she can begin to mourn his death; she has no relatives here with her and will stay away from the graveside (relatives don't attend the burial, by custom), gathering her few things together and preparing for the long, stunned walk home, a journey of two and a half days.

When the neat rectangular hole is little more than a foot deep, the men concentrate on digging a smaller, deeper hole, a grave within a grave, hacking away at the stony ground with an axe to straighten the sides. A man in a striped shirt, the father of the anemic boy, stands in the deeper hole to scoop out the last of the soil. The new inner grave is barely as wide as his two feet pressed together. Ismail picks out loose stones and measures the length again, checking everything over one last time before the tools are laid to one side and the men turn to face Lemun, the sky clouded darkly over now, the rain beginning to fall. The whole job has taken about an hour, and it's still such a small, small grave. It must be these fathers' wish—every parent's wish—never to have to do this for one of their own.

Another man appears down by the stream, walking quickly through the long, wet grass. He is carrying the child, Mustafa, wrapped in a printed blue sheet. The boy's body looks light and limp in the man's arms. His head falls down from the man's forearm, out of proportion with the rest of his body, his bound feet pointing away to one side. Together, the men hold Mustafa's body over the grave, unwinding the blue sheet, laying him into the ground, wrapped only in thin, white gauze. The grave is well measured, and he fits snugly into the hole. They place small, round stones onto his body and lay the flat rocks across to form a lid. They mix the water with soil to form a clay, plastering it over the rocks, and heap dry soil on top. The measuring stick is snapped in two and stuck at either end, the head and the foot. They crouch around the grave, tidying the mound, picking out stones and grass, patting it smooth. They wash their hands and sprinkle water onto the soil. They stand back, quietly, and Ismail mutters some words, almost inaudibly, the other men murmuring in agreement, briefly lifting their palms to the bruised and impassive sky before turning and walking away, ignoring the writer and photographer intruding on this small scene of ordinary sadness. They wash their hands again in the stream, hurrying to get back to the clinic before the clouds burst open.

MSF will be leaving Lemun soon. Their role here has been as specialists in emergency health care, and as hard as life in Nuba still undoubtedly is, it can no longer be described as an emergency. The clinics will be handed over to an organization more focused on development, training, and education, while MSF focuses its resources on the many ongoing emergencies elsewhere. The people of Nuba have come through many difficult years, and although food is still short, and children are still dying, they at last—hopefully, or *inshaallah*—have reason to look to the future. People are returning from long exiles, rebuilding their homes, replanting their fields, resurrecting the gatherings and markets and festivals they've been afraid to hold for so long.

Anil Osman had a story that was typical of many. Born in Lemun in 1975, he left home as an eleven-year-old ("because the situation it's a little bit severe at that time") and traveled with his brothers and sister to El Obeid, in the north. I asked him what he meant by the situation being a little bit severe, and he shrugged. "If they suspect you are a rebel they will come and take you, and if you are not lucky they will kill you. And if you are lucky, and you have cows, they will rather take cows." He lived in El Obeid with his brothers and sister, without word from their parents, finishing school, finding work, and marrying a childhood friend from Lemun who had also gone to El Obeid, until, with the first peace agreement being signed in 2002, he began to think about going back to Lemun. "I told my brother," he said, "now it looks a little bit safe, I have to go and see my mother and father, because we have been here a long time without seeing them, it will be better to see them if they are alive or where they live." He came alone first, leaving his wife and two children in El Obeid, wary of believing that the fragile ceasefire would hold. "Peace is like oxygen for life here," he told me. "We want to live, and without peace is not life." He found work with MSF, rebuilt a small house a few minutes' walk from the clinic, and watched the ceasefire being renewed two, three, four times. Soon, he said, he will send for his family and bring them home to live in Lemun.

I walked up to his house with him, and he showed me where he will build another one to make room for his wife and children, explaining how he will carry the stones to the site, cut the branches, dry the grasses for the roof. The end of the year is a good time for people to come back to Nuba, he said, because the building materials are in good supply. I stood by his doorway, looking down into the valley. I could just see the evening's football match being played out; and beyond that, women washing clothes at the stream. In the distance, I could see the small hillock where Mustafa had been buried. I asked Anil what he thought the valley would look like in the future. "Lots of changes," he said. "People will move from up hills to down, and they will receive a lot of development they don't have before. They will have hospitals, they will have more schools, they will have tarmac roads. I am happy to be here the rest of my life," he added. "That's why I want to bring my family back here in Nuba Mountains."

I remembered Mahamud, an MSF nurse, describing his return to Nuba after a fifteen-year absence. "It was a very big party," he said. "I was feeling very happy. Really very happy. It was as if someone was lost or was dead and had come again."

This is the hospital that MSF built in Lemun. There are no roads, so it is not uncommon for people to walk several days to reach the clinic, often having to carry the sick.

Previous spread, left: Many inhabitants of the villages in Nuba had to leave during the war. This young girl had recently returned to her home after being forced away.
Previous spread, right: A father walked for two days with his daughter to bring her to the MSF clinic in Lemun, where they waited together for medical care.

Below: A mother holding
her child, who has a fever
from malaria.

Right: When you walk through
the Nuba Mountains,
everybody stops to say hello.
This girl greeted us during our
ten-day walk.

Left: Sisters

Below: Wrapped in white cloth is the tiny body of a four-year-old boy named Mustafa Phillis. He was carried to the clinic by his mother, but the combination of malaria and malnutrition killed him. The screams of his mother were heart stopping. Only men attend funerals, so we accompanied the hospital orderly and a few men from the village who helped chip away at his little grave. As they filled in the broken ground over him, an angry black storm erupted over the gravesite. We filed back to camp in total silence in the pouring rain.

Uganda

The Good Doctors

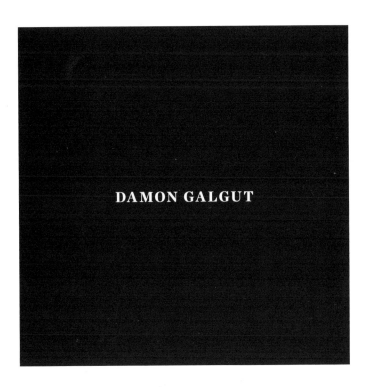

DAMON GALGUT

SAM ODANG* IS BATTLING WITH HIS DEMONS. He is only twenty, with an open, shiny face, but when I start talking to him his expression clouds over. He gets the hooded, hunted look I have started to recognize.

Sam was abducted by the Lord's Resistance Army (LRA) from his home in northern Uganda, along with his parents and seven others, in 1999. Soon after, he was forced to hack his mother and father to death with a machete. It was like a terrible dream, he says, from which he couldn't wake up. On the long walk to the LRA camp in Sudan, he helped kill another four people. That was just the start. He had a month's training, and then was given a gun and sent back to Uganda. They were a group of one hundred, under one commander, which then split into smaller groups with different functions. He had the job of killing. He killed soldiers, he killed civilians. He has, he says, killed "many people."

I press him, as gently as I can, on how many exactly. He only repeats it again—"many"—and shakes his head.

In September 2003 he decided to escape; he'd heard of an amnesty on the radio. The LRA trusted him by then, so it wasn't hard to get away. He buried his gun and gave himself up.

When he came back to his village, it was all right at first. But then the bad dreams came—dreams of shooting and killing, of endless running through the bush. There is a traditional ritual of return, in which a goat or chicken is slaughtered, but at first his village didn't perform this ritual for him. Then they did, and he felt a bit better. After six months he came for counseling at the clinic run by MSF in Aromo camp, but the nightmares and flashbacks continued. His counselor gave him a small job, weighing and measuring the babies who come in to the clinic, and it's been good for him. But he's still tormented and he's scared he may be abducted again; he would be killed immediately for having run away.

When I ask him how he feels about the future he shakes his head. All he wants, he says, is somebody to help him by taking the bad dreams away.

It would be nice to report that Sam's story is an aberration, a sick twist of fate that happened only to him. But the truth is that his experience is a common one. Aside from a core group of perhaps two hundred commanders, the LRA is made up entirely of kidnapped children who are used as porters and soldiers. Many of the girls, if they're not turned into fighters, are given as sex slaves to the commanders, who accumulate harems of "wives" to minister to them. Without exception, the abducted children witness acts of hideous violence, and most are forced to participate in them. Very often they are made to kill members of their own family or their friends. It is the LRA's way of inducting them into the movement, of making it impossible to return. Attempted escape is punishable by death, usually at the hands of a new "recruit" who has recently been captured.

Yet many of the children do escape, sometimes after years. The Rachele center in Lira town is a safe haven, a place of rehabilitation for some of these children. There are 130 of them at the moment, down from a high of 350. Most will stay for an average of two months, but some will stay much longer, and a few, who have no families to return to, will be here indefinitely.

Some of these children are playing in the dusty yard when we arrive, laughing and shouting and running. Their clothes are ragged, their feet bare—but that is not unusual in Africa. They look like any normal, happy group of kids. But every one of them has a story, and not one of the stories is good.

Simon* is a shy, good-looking boy of nineteen, resting on crutches, his one leg horribly swollen and discolored. He talks softly, looking down, never meeting my eyes. He tells me he was abducted by a group of rebels three years ago, along with three other children from his village. Like Sam, he was sent up to a camp in Sudan for military training, but a month later the Ugandan army (UPDF) bombed the camp, sending them back over the border. Simon took part in food raids, attacks on civilians, and the abduction of other children.

For a long time he was too scared to escape, until he was wounded in an army ambush, his leg badly shot up. Then he decided he had nothing to lose and, one night, when he was on guard duty, a little ways off from the others, he sneaked away. He hid his gun and gave himself up to the army. He had been told the UPDF would kill him, but instead they brought him here.

Then there is Linda*, who was abducted in 1996 when she was twelve years old. She was given as a "wife" to one of the LRA commanders and had a child by him one month ago. She smiles and looks down at her baby with love, though she says she never wants to see the father again. Many of the girls in the yard—all children themselves—are carrying babies, the product of LRA rape.

This savage insurgency has dragged on now for eighteen years. The LRA cannot possibly win, yet their campaign has been brutally effective: 1.6 million people (more than 80 percent of the local population) displaced from their homes and 100,000 killed. More than 20,000 children have been stolen.

So much slaughter and terror—to what end? It is sometimes hard to tell. Aside from a desire to overthrow the Ugandan government, Joseph Kony, the leader of the LRA, says he wants to establish a country based on the Ten Commandments. Number six, apparently, doesn't apply to him. And he has added some novel ones of his own: thou shalt not ride a bicycle, for example—a sin punishable by amputation. Thou shalt not breed pigs—punishable by death. He claims to receive instruction from the Holy Ghost, as well as various animist spirits. There is, in truth, nothing Christian about Kony, unless it is an Old Testament view of purgation through violence, with himself cast in the role of God.

It is tempting, even consoling, to dismiss him as a madman. But there is a diabolical logic to this lunacy. An army made up of abducted children can be endlessly replenished. Children are pliant and vulnerable, easily controlled.

At the same time, his methods are self-defeating. Kony is from the Acholi, a northern people who have long been at odds with the center of power down south in Kampala. This is a schism with deep historical roots, going back at least as far as colonial times. But the current war grew out of a series of insurgencies that started in 1986 when President Museveni reneged on a power-sharing deal with General Tito Okello, an Acholi. Pushed from power, remnants of Okello's army joined in Sudan with some Acholi politicians and ex–Idi Amin soldiers to form the Uganda Peoples Democratic Army (UPDA). The new regime in Kampala managed to neutralize the threat with a peace deal, but another rebellion took shape in the form of the Holy Spirit Movement (HSM) of Alice Auma "Lakwena." With massive popular support, the HSM swept southward almost to the capital, but they were militarily defeated. Lakwena's father tried to rouse the movement again, using terror tactics against children for the first time, but the momentum of revolt had run out. In the vacuum that followed, Kony—a former UPDA commander who had also tried to take over the HSM—stepped in.

Among the Acholi there is a general mistrust and resentment of the Museveni government, and the feeling appears to be mutual. It is a situation, you might think, ripe with revolutionary potential—and yet Kony has blown it. He claims to be fighting for the Acholi people, but since 1991, when some civilian militias were raised against him, they have become his victims. They must be punished, he says, for turning against him. So it is their children he steals, their homes he burns, their lives he destroys.

MSF runs a therapeutic feeding center in Lira town, opened a year ago, to care for children under five. The scene is a sun-baked compound, perhaps half a kilometer square. In the middle are fifteen concrete buildings with zinc roofs. In the shade inside, mothers and their children lie on thin mattresses under mosquito nets. Chickens scratch in the dirt, and brightly colored clothes are drying on the grass. There is a curious mixture of idleness and activity, giving again that strange illusion of normality.

But look closely. This little girl has a hugely swollen belly, and her hair is an odd color. The tiny boy over there is like a skeleton with skin, his eyes unnaturally huge in his face. The gaze of this one is dull and listless, that one too electric and aware. These are all signs of malnutrition, which takes the forms of either wasting or distension.

I speak to a few of the mothers. Susan Apio is here with her one-year-old son, Innocent, who's still breast-feeding. She recently moved from her village to a "protected camp," where as yet no aid organizations are providing food. The little she did have was stolen by the rebels. Innocent fell gravely ill, and she traveled for one day to bring him here. He has improved greatly, she says; he can crawl again now, whereas before he wasn't moving at all. But when I ask what she will do to feed him when she goes back to the camp, she shrugs. She will try to get work, she tells me, to pay for food, but she says this without much conviction.

Malnourishment lowers the immune system, which is when opportunistic infections like TB spring up. So there is a special TB ward here too, with fifteen children, and an intensive-care ward, where more extreme conditions—malaria, respiratory illnesses, dehydration—receive twenty-four-hour care. There is also a supplementary feeding scheme, where about four hundred children whose state is not yet critical come as outpatients. There are 150 children on the therapeutic feeding scheme at the moment—down from four hundred last year. It's a good sign.

Lira is a big town, and there is safety in numbers. But traditional life up here used to center on small villages—a few huts, some fields and cattle. A subsistence economy, not abundant, but enough. The war has changed all that.

The government ordered all civilians into camps in 1996, ostensibly to protect them better. But the LRA continues to attack them there, and the army often preys on them too: there is a high incidence of rape.

I drive out to Aromo camp. It's a drive of an hour on pot-holed dirt roads. Occasionally the simmering bush opens out to show abandoned settlements—schools, churches, houses, all empty now. There are some people on the road, or working a field here and there, but all of them will be gone by dark.

Most of the other aid organizations travel under armed guard. But MSF believes it is safer to be unarmed; weapons announce that you have something to defend. They radio in every twenty minutes and stop to ask soldiers or civilians whether the road ahead is safe. No other precautions, and so far it's worked, except that last week an MSF car was shot up and looted by two teenagers, miraculously without anyone being killed. But everyone hopes it was banditry and not the LRA—a small, theoretical comfort.

We get to Aromo without incident. "Camp" is hardly the word: it's a vast, congested, teeming conglomeration of huts, built almost on top of each other. There are about 26,000 people here, and it's still expanding. When fire breaks out here—which it frequently does—it leaps rapidly between the thatched roofs. No less lethal or fast is the spread of disease, one of the reasons why we are here.

The clinic itself is right at the edge of the camp, where nobody wants to be; the center is the safest. The area is known for rebel activity; bands of rebels are sometimes spotted passing nearby. The army has set up a small barracks next door—a line of huts dug in below ground level, to protect against bullets. But the view from the clinic verandah is peaceful: under a mango tree a line of patients is being registered at a table, babies are being weighed and measured in a sling hung from a branch. Beyond an umber vista of open fields there is a fringe of bush in the distance.

Karen, the MSF doctor on duty, carries out consultations with the help of a local translator. Most sessions last less than five minutes. The first patient is a little girl with fever and diarrhea. But she also has a mouth infection, which must first be treated before any underlying illness can be found. Her mother is given a prescription and sent to the pharmacy next door. Then there is a child with worms, easily diagnosed and treated. Then a girl who's been operated on by a traditional healer, who performed a tonsillectomy with a bicycle spoke. Not surprisingly, the wound has turned septic.

The next case is rather more sensational: a thirteen-year-old boy possessed by demons. Or so says his uncle, who has been praying over him at the church. His state is certainly alarming: he is unconscious, but when his blood is taken he starts up, snapping and convulsing and drooling, his eyes crossed. Four people have to hold him down. It started very suddenly two days ago, the uncle says. His face is full of fear, and when I speak to him, it's easy to understand why: six of the boy's siblings have already died of malaria, as have three of the uncle's own children. The boy's father was killed by the LRA a year ago.

Karen suspects cerebral malaria. She does a paracheck on him, which is an ingenious little test that allows for a very rapid diagnosis. But it's only valid for certain types of malaria, so when the test comes back negative she sends his blood away to the lab to be checked again. Meanwhile she has started him on an antibiotic for meningitis, which she now suspects is the problem.

But her first suspicion is correct: in the lab, Richard, a member of the national staff, shows me the little malaria parasites under the microscope. Karen starts him on treatment immediately. The national treatment here is with fansidar and chloriquine, but the local strain of malaria is resistant, so MSF uses artesunate and amodiaquine. It's very effective, but this little boy has been brought in very late. Perhaps too late.

He sleeps that night in the compound with us: every hour or two his anguished cries ring out, mingling with the sounds of cows and goats. In the morning he is much quieter but still unconscious; Karen rates his chances at fifty-fifty. That little boy becomes some sort of symbol for me, and it's almost a personal relief to hear, a few days later, that he is eating and conscious and back at home again.

The clinic also has a health education department, which uses twelve outreach workers who go through the camp, teaching people about issues like hygiene, water, and sanitation. And there is a mental health counselor, Olga Akello, who runs group therapy and individual counseling sessions with abducted children and their parents. "The social network systems have disintegrated," she says. I don't envy her work, but she is upbeat and positive. The Acholi culture is one of forgiveness and reconciliation, she says; she uses rituals of traditional cleansing and prayer to help communities accept abducted children.

From the social worker at the Rachele center I heard the same bright message. But is it true? No matter how accommodating a culture may be, there are some horrors, surely, it's impossible to forget. Even more worrying, how possible is it for children, steeped in years of violence, to live out a different pattern when they come back? While I'm there, I hear at least two terrible stories about children who've returned from the bush: in one, a boy poured paraffin over his baby brother and set him alight. In the other a boy, whose little sister complained about having to carry a heavy load, lost his mind and beat her to death. Then some people from the community arrived and beat him to death in turn.

The father north you go, the older the war is. Right up near the border, around Kitgum, is where the trouble first began.

The MSF operation up here is more basic. The clinic in Atanga camp, for example, has only one room: a long concrete shed, one corner of which has been partioned off with bamboo screens for consultations. There is the same procession of infections and minor injuries, reassuring in their mildness.

In the square outside, in the shade of three mango trees, a big meeting is in progress. A government delegation has come to speak to the community. A crowd of a few hundred murmurs responsively as they listen to two military officers, their message conveyed by an animated translator. It feels like a charismatic church gathering, but the substance of it seems to be an appeal: "there is light at the end of the tunnel. If you have any information about the LRA, share it with us."

Then a bespectacled lady with a high-pitched voice comes forward. She is introduced as the "minister of state for northern Ugandan rehabilitation and development." She is vigorous and enthusiastic, acting out her points with mime and gesture:

"While the rest of Uganda has been going like this"—she walks boldly forward—"Acholiland is going like this"—she walks backward. "If you could go there, you would see Kampala is glittering"—she flutters her hands emphatically. "In Kampala, we eat and dance all night! In Kampala, you can struggle and make life better for yourself. Here in Acholiland, there is suffering and grief."

Then she makes a big promise of money "to get Acholiland walking like this"—she does her forward stride again. "Peace is coming. The Ugandan government is trying to get our brothers to come out of the bush. We want to bring a better life for you. For this one, a better life"—she picks up a baby, who bursts immediately into a wail, setting off general laughter.

The next speaker is a "turned" LRA commander, an older man with silver hair, who launches into a loud speech in Acholi. It's a telling irony that he is the first one, in this gathering, to address these people in their own language.

Peace is coming. The government has been saying that for a long time. The message is being repeated vehemently of late, because there are new initiatives in the air: until recently, Sudan and Uganda were both providing weapons and shelter to each other's insurgencies, but that's all off now. Cause for hope? Maybe, but not one Acholi I spoke to believes it. The common perception seems to be that it's in the interests of the Museveni government to keep the LRA on the boil, because without them the Acholi might consolidate into a real threat.

It's hard not to have some sympathy with this view. An insurgency that's dragged on for eighteen years? A rebel army with no willing recruits, yet the government can't protect its citizens? You have to suspect the political will for resolution. And the next day, walking through the camp, we come across a small gathering of mourners. They tell us that three men, who had left the camp to go hunting, were killed by the LRA a few days ago. They want to bury their dead, but the army refuses to retrieve the bodies: there are too many rebels out there, they say. It's too dangerous.

Too dangerous? Too many rebels? These are the same army commanders we heard under the mango tree, appealing for information and help from the people. They're supposed to be looking for the rebels.

Maurina Lakang, Agnes Akeny, Angella Ladyer, Scovia Akan, Grace Aduk, Silvia Acan, Elda Akwero, Santa Akwero. These names are unlikely to make any big mark on history. They belong to a group of women who lived ordinary lives, until everything changed for them last week.

We sit on the grass outside the Kitgum hospital buildings while they tell their story in little fragments, overlapping each other. I notice that, unlike the abducted children I've listened to, they look directly at me while they speak. I'm the one who looks away, at my hands, my pen, anything rather than their faces.

Yet the horror is hidden behind clean, white bandages, through which they even manage to smile and joke softly.

A week ago they left Ngomoromo camp, near the Sudanese border, where they live, to collect water from a stream about two miles away. On the way they were ambushed by a group of rebels—three men and two boys—who made them start walking toward some abandoned buildings farther off. One of the women, Alimina Adyer, had a small baby who started crying. The rebels ripped the baby from its mother's arms and killed it with a rifle butt. The mother, who couldn't bear to watch, tried to run away; they battered her to death too. The other women were forced into an empty house. Now they were going to punish them for not listening, the rebels said, and if any of them made a sound, they would be killed too. Then they cut off their lips, one by one, with a bayonet. They tore off their clothes and told them to run back to their "husbands," meaning the army, and show them what had happened.

When they finish talking a silence falls, in which I am scrabbling for something to say. It's only afterward that it occurs to me: that little speechless gap is the only proper response. Any questions, any abstract political philosophies, have no purchase here. There is a level on which this violence has no reason or purpose; it exists to gratify itself. Pain for the sake of power.

On the way out, our translator, David, points to the verandah of the hospital. "Many night commuters will come," he says. "In one hour, two hours, they will be here."

Night commuter—part of the sick parlance of the war. It refers to thousands and thousands of people, mostly children, who each night walk for miles to the center of the towns and camps to sleep, away from the danger at the edges.

"This whole place will be full of them," David says.

For a moment I imagine it: the rows of bodies lined up, sleeping and breathing in the dark. They will be here until the sun rises, then they will get up and walk back to where they came from, to go on with the business of their lives.

*Names have been changed.

Heavy rains in Lord's
Resistance Army territory.

This is the spot where Speke
identified the source of the Nile
in 1862.

Below: A sandstorm in Kitgum.   *Right:* Children run after our vehicle at the camp in Aromo.

Villagers leave the Aromo camp in the morning to work in the fields and bush. At the time it was surrounded by Lord's Resistance Army positions, so venturing any distance from the camp was potentially very dangerous.

Below: The Lord's Resistance Army had consistently used mutilation and horrific acts of violence as part of their reign of terror in Northern Uganda. The LRA caught this group of women as they were collecting water, killing a mother and her baby with their rifle butts. In an act of unthinkable and inhuman brutality, they cut the lips off all the other women with their bayonets.

Right: A camp for former child soldiers and young members of the Lord's Resistance Army.

The Ukraine

Are We Leaving Already?

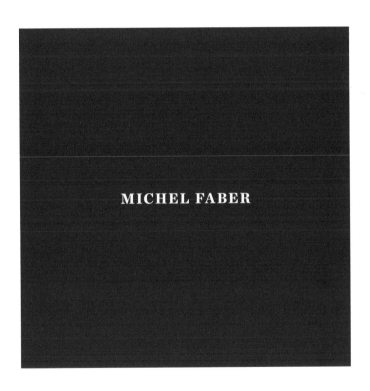

MICHEL FABER

ODESSA, SO THE TOURIST BROCHURES SAY, is the pearl of the Black Sea, the Palmiras of the North. It's romantic and vibrant and intoxicating. The city's women are famously beautiful. Visit the many websites offering mail-order Ukrainian "brides" and you can view a selection of "hot sexy" ones frolicking on Odessa's unspoiled beaches. Arranged meetings with seventeen- to twenty-three-year-olds cost eighty-nine American dollars, twenty-four- to thirty-year-olds are seventy-nine dollars, while women over forty-one are a bargain at fifty-nine dollars. All females are "guaranteed available"; any that might cause disappointment are instantly deleted.

Once upon a time, Ukraine was a communist state in which enterprises like this were inconceivable, but in which thousands of people got "deleted" for real. The country has a brutal history of Stalinist purges and oppression. Since the collapse of the Soviet Union in 1992, it has striven to become a European democracy. As in other post-Soviet states, the results have been a mix of inspirational achievements and dispiriting betrayals. There are elections, with the usual controversies about vote-rigging and shady candidates. The economy is on the up. There is an emergent middle class, free at last to travel, free to think and do all sorts of things that were previously forbidden. Prada and McDonalds have set up shop amid the shabby tenements and derelict palaces. Every day, more billboards are erected and more imports become available. But one of the biggest imports since the mid-nineties has been HIV/AIDS. An estimated 400,000 people are infected, or roughly 1 percent of the sexually active population. It's a bigger time bomb than Chernobyl.

I'm in Odessa with Médecins Sans Frontières, an organization better known for its interventions in African war zones and famine camps. We're in a restaurant, eating a nice breakfast of cherry pancakes. Outside on Deribasovskaya Street, a revolving advertisement for a bride agency winks at us through the window. Natalia Rudaya, MSF's PR officer, is explaining that getting interviews and pictures for my article will be difficult. The epidemic is, well, kind of a secret. Over the last four years, MSF's attempts to help the local health care system come to grips with it have been hampered by denial, ignorance, and fear. There is a terrible stigma around HIV. Sufferers who are well enough to live at home anxiously conceal their status from neighbors, flatmates, even family members. The terminally ill are kept in conditions the Ministry of Health would rather not advertise. And then there are the obstacles of official accreditations and permissions, stamps, and signatures. Natalia sighs in frustration.

One person who proves unusually willing to talk is Ludmila Urmanzhy, a sixty-two-year-old woman we meet at the Outpatients

Department of the Regional Infectious Diseases Hospital. Ludmila has traveled a long way with her ten-month-old grandson, Ilya; the clinic is in the middle of nowhere, behind a Jewish cemetery, flanked by decaying factories. But Ludmila is motivated because her grandson has AIDS and the doctors have just started him on the anti-retroviral (ARV) drugs that may keep him alive.

Ludmila used to be a technologist in a baby food factory. Now, in a cruel irony, she relies on handouts of infant formula. She also gratefully accepts a jumbo pack of disposable diapers; they're the wrong size for little Ilyousha, but the clinic hasn't got any smaller ones. I ask Ludmila when her life started to go wrong, and she erupts into a passionate tirade against her useless son, his junkie girlfriend, and the social catastrophe that has engulfed Ukraine since the collapse of the Soviet Union. Like many disaffected pensioners, Ludmila appears to have forgotten some of the horrors of Stalinism, remembering instead the way the old regime took responsibility for its citizens' welfare. She yells and weeps and shakes her fists, incensed that she's been reduced to hawking cigarettes in the street, unable even to afford a cot for her grandchild. "He's all I've got in my life now," she says. "This baby."

As for the possibility of me and Tom accompanying her to her home and taking pictures, she's all for it. "You're very welcome. I'm not afraid of anything. I don't give a shit where this article will be published. People should speak out." Mention of the imminent election triggers another diatribe against corrupt politicians. "Who is prosperous in this country?" she cries. "Only thieves and bandits!"

On the long, bone-shaking bus journey from the AIDS clinic to her home, Ludmila begins to get nervous. Her righteous fury is spent, giving way to jitters about the possible consequences of this encounter with foreigners. By the time we get to her flat, she demands a signed document promising that my article will not be published in Ukraine. I sit on the bed next to the sick baby, scribbling two contracts on official-looking letterhead from an Italian B&B—one for her, one for us. Even so, she insists we can only take photographs in her bedroom. The rest of her home—a dark, grimy lounge dominated by a broken carriage and a balcony on which the baby's wretched father stands smoking—is off limits. The interview is cut short when Ilya, an enchantingly good-natured, trusting child, needs his afternoon enema.

Fighting for the lives of those already infected is important, but prevention is naturally the greater aim. A wondrous variety of aid organizations and charities, both international and homegrown, are at work in Ukraine to keep vulnerable people from contracting the disease. They include Faith Hope Love, which focuses its attention on addicts and sex workers, and Life Plus, which offers counseling, education, and other support for homosexuals. Tom and I spend a night hanging around Odessa's dock district, waiting for a chance to talk to prostitutes who aren't interested in the kind of conversation I want to have and who won't be photographed. Then I spend a frustrating afternoon talking to young homosexuals whose magnificently sad stories I already know won't fit into the article.

Then I talk to some of MSF's peer counselors—people who have experience with HIV and are willing to share their stories with those for whom it's a terrifying unknown. Ukraine's health care service is full of specialists but has no equivalent of the family GP, so a bit of compassionate advice when you first realize you're sick is hard to come by. Peer counselors offer this, combating the syndrome of fear and shame that makes infected people reluctant to seek help until it's too late. When it comes to preventing transmission of the virus from mother to child, a few weeks can make all the difference between a short-term challenge and a lifelong tragedy.

Oxana Bevzuk is a peer counselor who is HIV-positive. Her nineteen-month-old baby Nikolai has AIDS. Oxana's beauty, smart clothes, high heels, and general air of chic give no clue to the conditions in which she lives: a "communalka" whose kitchen, toilet, and bathroom she shares with four other families, and whose tiny living room has space for little more than a couch bed. The makeup and hairbrushes with which Oxana keeps herself so impeccably groomed nestle in a sink the size of a military helmet. Her older son, a ten-year-old, has to sleep on the floor; we never meet him, as he hasn't been told of his baby brother's illness. Oxana's beloved parents don't know either. She explains that she doesn't want to worry them; her father's unwell, her mother is overworked, and so on. Still, Oxana risks stigma enough by agreeing to be photographed in the public park near her home. Passersby stare curiously at this elegant young woman posing with her child. Why all the fuss? Who are these foreigners? What's this woman got that we haven't got?

Health care in Ukraine is supposedly free, but in practice patients pay, and HIV patients pay more than most. The going rate for a caesarean (essential to prevent transmission of the virus to newborn babies) is $300, unless you're HIV-positive, in which case it's $500. One AIDS sufferer recalls how, when he needed an operation for septic pneumonia, he was required to supply his own surgical instruments. Pitifully unwell, he'd traipsed around the city with a medical shopping list, searching for hard-to-find items like 100ml syringes and disposable scissors.

It is just about true that in Ukraine, you can get anything if you're willing to pay. Unfortunately this principle goes beyond the usual goods and services and extends into complicated patterns of bribery. Tom is hampered by his determination to tread an honorable path through a moral morass. We hear, for example, of a notorious heroin addict who, for twenty dollars, will inject for the camera. "They were so happy," our interpreter says of a German TV crew who handed over the twenty and filmed the needle going in. When we debate the moral implications of degradation-for-cash, she seems to feel we're out of touch with reality. "Of course they paid. The Germans pay. The Dutch pay. The Canadians pay. Everybody pays."

Unsurprisingly, some of Odessa's beggars have wised up to what foreign journalists expect of them. On one visit to a dusty junkyard that's home to a community of urchins, several boys leap around excitedly, crying "Money! Money! Money!" and miming the clicking of cameras. One boy assumes a picturesque pose of misery, hiding his tousled head inside his jacket, peeping out to see if that's what's wanted. Another snatches a plastic bag out of the trash and puffs it against his face to indicate glue sniffing. Shameless imposture? Yes, except that these kids do sniff glue, and they are genuinely destitute. They're only hamming up their real life.

One local aid organization that understands street kids well is The Way Home. Their director, Sergey Kostin, confirms that homelessness practically didn't exist in Soviet times; indeed, under Stalinist surveillance, it was almost impossible. Troubled youngsters and runaways were assimilated into social clubs tacitly supported by the state, but these were scrapped when communism ended. Now the homeless population in Odessa has swelled to many thousands, and The Way Home is doing its best to rescue some of them from starvation, drug abuse, and infectious diseases. As well as distributing food, clothing, and first aid, and providing a shelter for a motley assortment of youngsters, The Way Home publishes the Ukrainian equivalent of *The Big Issue* and is currently building a leisure center. "We're trying to restore the former Soviet Union system," Kostin says, only half-joking.

The Way Home's shelter is an extraordinary testament to what can be achieved with obstinate zeal, positive energy, and bags of kindness. Team leaders Raisa Krayeva and Dmitry Rzhepishersky describe their role laughingly—but accurately—as "mother figure" and "father figure." The kids who live with them are all refugees from alcoholic, neglectful, or mysteriously vanished parents; Raisa and Dmitry fill the void with no-nonsense grace. The kids are taught to help each other; one month they're street trash, the next they're fledgling social workers, patrolling their old haunts to offer buns, bandages, and a chat.

When I ask these children to discuss their hopes for a better future, their answers are humbly realistic. Vera, a sweet, pretty fourteen-year-old, would like to finish school and work in a bar like her mum. Eighteen-year-old Sasha wants to be a better busker and plays me a couple of songs on a rubbish-skip guitar mended with sticky tape. Rustem wants to see *Lord of the Rings* or *Harry Potter*. None of these kids has fantasies of being models or movie stars. Their most starry-eyed ambition is a university education. In the meantime, they're enjoying building their leisure center, hammering in the nails, balancing on the roofbeams with no visible means of support.

One sunny afternoon, we pile into The Way Home van and accompany the team on their daily rounds of homeless communities. First stop is the Odessa steps, a tourist hot spot where lovers kiss in front of the statue of Pushkin and holidaymakers admire the docks below. A quick walk through the adjacent park brings us to a homeless crew who've colonized a small, concrete storehouse formerly used for buckets, mops, and other janitorial equipment. I ask our interpreter the meaning of the graffiti that is sprayed under the bas-relief sculpture of Gorky. "It's slang," she says. "But something like 'death' or 'the end.'"

Inside the storeroom, five youngsters are sleeping in opiated serenity. Two boys, Igor and Andrej, both fifteen, share the same mattress, oblivious to us or the rat that scampers around them. Fluffy toys, pictures of kittens, and pages torn from a coloring book are littered around, for this shelter has been home to small children too. A broken cassette machine is loaded with Acid Euro Trance 5, but the air is tranquil, punctuated only by the occasional toot or tannoy announcement from the docks.

Outside in another concrete cubbyhole, Yana is already awake. She's eighteen, somewhat scabby-faced, her hair peppered with dandelion. Dmitry gives her a cigarette and a light, and she smiles. Her teeth are bad—a long-term drug addict's teeth. Raisa scolds her for running away from the hospital again, but Yana protests languidly that she gets bored there. Raisa bemoans the passing of Soviet times, when nobody could "escape" from hospital, especially someone like Yana, who has syphilis. Later that evening, Tom will spot this girl in the city center, perched in a shop window.

Next stop on The Way Home's tour of bandage and bun distribution is the ruins of a bulldozed apartment block in the middle of the city. Fenced off from the urban bustle all around, we literally stumble upon a scene of utter devastation, an apt symbol of the collapsed infrastructure of post-Soviet Ukraine. The ruins are surrounded by mounds of garbage: rotting watermelon slices, broken bottles, the rubber flap of a turntable, dog shit, printed circuits, the empty foils of prescription drugs, smashed furniture. While squatting on a pile of lumber, I notice, in the tangle of wood under my feet, a dusty, half-rotted, half-mummified kitten. Just one room of the apartment block has survived semi-intact. Half-buried in earth, the chamber is more like a cave. Crows caw overhead. "This is social Armageddon," murmurs Tom as the narcotized inhabitants clamber out of their burrow.

Twenty-six-year-old Lena holds out a grotesquely swollen, abscessed hand that resembles a baby rhinoceros head with a winking eye. She is listless as Dmitry smears a Marmite-like substance on a clean bandage and applies it to the wound. What this woman really needs is hospitalization, fast, but that's not realistic. Reality for these people is their grubby community, in which the proceeds from begging and prostitution are pooled in vats of homemade Voltushka, an ephedrine-based stimulant they inject every few hours.

Dmitry squats next to an emaciated girl called Nina. Unlike most of Odessa's homeless, who come from unemployment-racked rural villages, or from Moldova, or from that strange self-proclaimed, unrecognized republic Pridnestrovye, she's actually from Odessa. She ran away from home because she and her stepfather didn't get along. She's twelve, and the bandage covering her infected track marks is filthy. Dmitry gives her a fresh one, writes her details into a Winnie the Pooh notebook, and invites her to come to The Way Home. Maybe another day, Nina says. Not today.

Raisa promises to return in the morning, after ten, with a doctor and a pair of tennis shoes. We pick our way back through the rubble toward the van. The children wave goodbye. "Are we leaving already?" asks the interpreter. Yes, we're leaving. Tom's camera goes wheeep one last time. My Dictaphone squeals to a stop.

Ukraine, bolstered for so long by Soviet triumphalism and hopeful of a bright European future, understandably doesn't want to consider itself a disaster zone. The presence of foreign aid workers is an implicit reproach, a public embarrassment which, in theory, should spur the authorities into action. But in some ways, it's harder to get things done in a governmental bureaucracy than in a chaotic, famine-ridden war zone. In a war zone, you can pitch your tent and provide emergency medical care. In Ukraine, everything is supposed to be done via the existing health infrastructure—a system creakingly unaccustomed to change. Even small requests, such as an order for blood or a prescription for painkillers, must be approved by officials. Frustration with red tape regularly drives some doctors—against their ideological scruples—

to nip around to the local pharmacy and, out of their own pockets, buy what patients urgently need.

MSF is not here to stay; it's not a touring NHS. But Alexander Thissen, one of the expat doctors, is worried, like many people in the organization, about what will happen when the five-year mission in Ukraine is terminated. The term "exit strategy" is a controversial one in the midst of what is arguably still an emergency. Thissen is inclined to stay longer. We meet him as he and his Ukrainian colleague Aleksandr Telnov do their rounds at the Inpatients Department of the Regional Infectious Diseases Clinic. It's an impressive-sounding title for an ill-provisioned, shabby place that has the ambience of an old chemical warehouse. Until six months ago, the inmates were housed in a military-style complex complete with barbed wire, but a renovation grant from foreign donors was used as a pretext to evict everyone. After much lobbying, they were finally resettled here.

In Thissen's view, the relocation was a downward move. At least the previous facility, with its three-foot-thick walls, was easy to keep warm in winter and cool in summer. It was also run with a degree of autonomy. Here, bureaucracy is more obstructive. Staff and patients alike are aware they've been dumped in a place nobody else wanted. Morale has been low, and understaffing is acute. Nominally, there's a doctor on duty 24/7 but at nights this may be an elderly dentist who knows nothing about AIDS. The nurses, who cook as well, are assisted in their labors by the few relatives who haven't disowned their tainted offspring.

The men's ward is cluttered with dirty cups, cigarettes, buns, old paperbacks, a tiny portable TV, and human beings beyond saving. One, with sores all over his face and a towel wrapped around his head, groans loudly as mounting intracranial pressure causes him unbearable agony. His feet churn the bedclothes. The man in the adjacent bed is perturbed to see me kneeling on the floor; he motions me to take a proper seat. An old lady who has been tenderly massaging her son's hand gets up to show me a spread of clean newspaper I can sit on. In the corridor, patients squeeze their exhausted bodies back against the wall for fear of inconveniencing me as I pass by. I'm a visitor, after all, not a pariah like them.

In the women's ward, a string of washed white socks hangs drying across a high window. Who put them up there? Not Diane, who sits sorting her makeup drawer, rearranging her nail files and old family photographs. She's paralyzed from the waist down. Not Oxana, the wizened crone who lies staring at her bedside table with its jar of honey. She's too frail, must be about seventy. (I later learn she's twenty-three.) Maybe the socks were pinned up by Tanya, the hefty woman whom the doctors describe as a medical miracle. She should have been dead many times over. Maybe her former job—carrying bricks—has something to do with her survival. Thissen recalls her doing push-ups on the ward floor, trying to stay in shape, while her friends faded away. Mind you, Tanya's in chronic pain, her flesh scabby from an allergy to ARV drugs. There's a pathogen called Cryptococcus patiently waiting in her spinal fluid. She won't defy the odds forever.

One cell-like room has recently been allocated to those about to die. I sit on a bed stripped down to the bare metal wire and look upon a human skeleton in a blue nappy. He stares at the wall. His heart beats in his withered abdomen. There is nothing to say. His roommate, Igor, less close to death, motions me toward a chair. I want to ask Igor something, but by the time an interpreter is ready to help me I've no longer got what it takes. So, with only a mute gesture of farewell, I leave this polite, patient man to get on with his day's activities: waiting to feel worse, listening to the sounds of labored breathing and the cars passing outside.

Dr. Thissen vacillates between expressing his frustration with the system and worrying that I'll come away with too grim an impression. He's optimistic about the HIV situation in Ukraine, he assures me. This particular hospital is as bad as it gets; other places are much better. He's full of praise for the AIDS clinic in Mikolayev, a satellite city about 100 kilometers from Odessa. Not only are the buildings cleaner and better maintained, but Ministry of Health staff are dedicated and open-minded. He describes the training sessions that MSF conducts in the southern part of the country. "It's incredible, it's fantastic. We'll have an audience of forty, fifty doctors, and they literally suck up the information that we share with them. We did a session in an industrial city called Krivoj Rog. There were sixty people in the classroom, in impossibly hot conditions. They didn't even want to break for refreshments, they just wanted to keep going. They wanted to know it all."

In Odessa, however, the struggle has been uphill. MSF has often felt itself only grudgingly "tolerated." But, on the day we visit the hospital, Dr. Thissen's despondency is lifted by a wonderful coincidence, or perhaps a sign of things to come. A new Ministry of Health doctor has turned up for duty—a woman. Thissen and Telnov can't believe how much time she's spending with each patient, and how humanely she treats them. Instead of shutting herself in the office and scribbling reports, she's engaging with individuals, touching them. "She cares, you can tell," says Thissen. "A doctor like that would make a huge difference here."

In the immediate future, so much depends on the difference these homegrown individuals can make—how many of them emerge, and how many of them stick around to change the status quo. It's a terrifying time for HIV-positive people, who've been educated to understand the importance of strict adherence to drug therapy but are worried about future supplies being blocked by bureaucratic inefficiency or corruption. Oxana knows only too well what an interruption of ARV treatment would mean to her and her child. Another peer counselor, Julia, is aghast at the prospect of MSF's departure, and not just because she will lose a decently paid job in a country where decently paid jobs are scarce. "Who will take care of our patients?" she asks. "Just when we've worked out the best ways to tackle the problems, we have to go. We need more time, just a little more time. I'm afraid that everything will collapse as soon as we leave. This model we've created, it's too weak, the governmental health care system isn't ready to adopt it." Like a newborn child who's not ready to leave its mother, I suggest. Julia smiles. "Exactly. It's our baby."

But the baby has to be handed over. And it will be, soon. With any luck, the world will be watching to see what happens next, and Ukraine's health system will take charge, earning the admiration of us all. Let's just hope there's some money left after the country has hosted the next Eurovision Song Contest. In Kiev, a city already owing $350,000,000 in foreign debt, work has begun on several new five-star hotels for the expected influx of visitors. In the years ahead, even an epidemic like HIV/AIDS may be easier to roll back than the opportunistic invasion of Western-style capitalism. So far this infectious ideology has brought dubious thrills and alarming side effects. The weary hope is that eventually, some sort of equilibrium may come: a little more accountability at the top, a little less calamity at the bottom, something slightly better than constant frustration for those caught in between.

Right now, maybe Ukraine's current situation is summed up best not by an aid worker, but by the amiable American entrepreneur who rented us accommodation when MSF was turfed out of its old guesthouse. "It's a great country," he said, ushering us into a bedroom whose leopard-skin décor suggested it might be useful for his wife's dating agency. "Great people. Great opportunities. Unless you live here, right? Then it's not so great. But it's getting there. You gotta admit, it's getting there."

Two homeless boys, high on glue and a homemade cocktail of drugs, are passed out together in a makeshift squat in one of the parks of Odessa.

A homeless girl and her cat
wake up in a squat in Odessa.

Nina, a twelve-year-old runaway, regularly injects a concoction of drugs cooked up in a communal bowl that the inhabitants of this rubbish dump dip their needles into. It was hard not to think that things could have been different for this bright, pretty, and brave young girl.

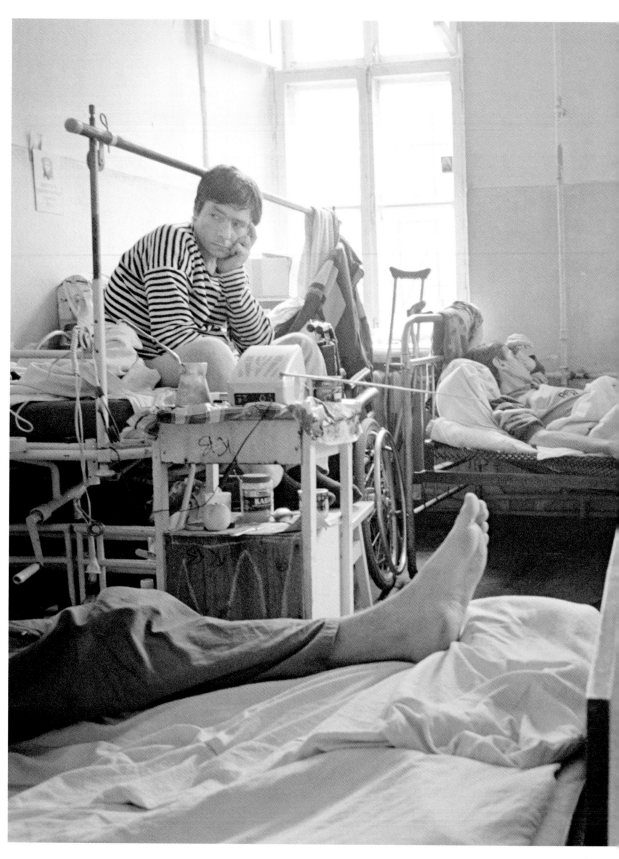

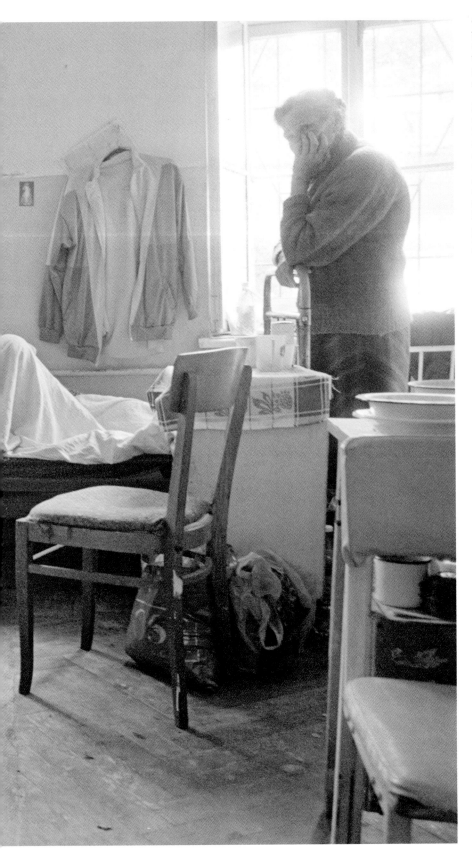

The issue of HIV has not been properly addressed in the Ukrainian health system. When we finally got access to one of the wards it seemed almost Dickensian.

Following spread, top left: One of the homeless boys visiting The Way Home, an amazing center that provides much-needed care for the homeless children of Odessa.
Bottom left: One of the patients on the HIV ward, tucked away and forgotten in a state hospital in Odessa.
Right: A homeless girl in her makeshift squat in an Odessa park.

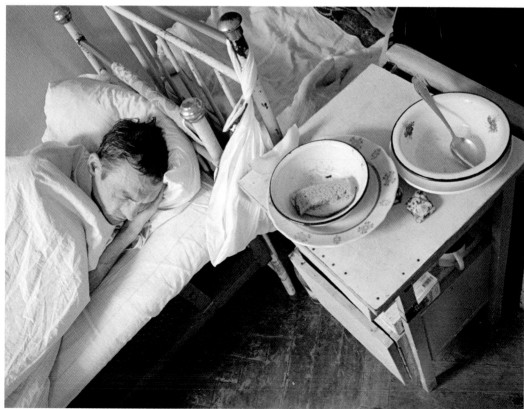

Uzbekistan

Disco Shoes and a Missing Sea

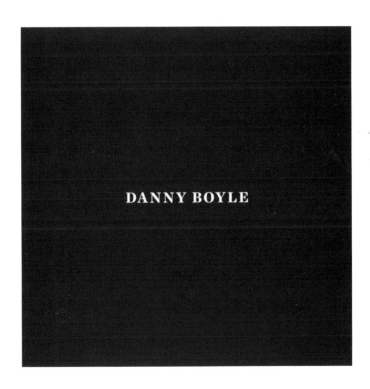

DANNY BOYLE

AS I WAS ARRIVING AT TASHKENT AIRPORT at 4 a.m., one of the first things I noticed was shoes. Our connection, a burly soldier with the build of an Uzbek Olympic wrestler, yawned and pointed us toward passport control. I looked down and saw that, at odds with his camouflage kit, were twinkling black plastic disco shoes. Intrigued, I noticed that the junior lost-luggage advisor had made her own footwear, or rather customized it by nailing wooden blocks to the heels. Later in the morning, I spotted another woman balanced on the highest heels I had ever seen outside of a porn film, and businessmen with beautifully turned-up toes, which pointed the tips at their owners' noses.

And later still, as we boarded an Anatonov 24—an "egg-beater" propeller plane—the airhostess wore shoes reminiscent of a Roxy Music album cover. But perhaps by this time I was following my interest in Uzbek shoe fashion in order to distract myself from something I had heard about Russian pilots: that prior to takeoff they fully clasp their vodka glasses with their fists, so that as they toast to the success of the flight, there's no chance of the clink being heard by passengers over the intercom. Na Zdovorie!

Out the window the buildings of Tashkent trickle into sand.

Once upon a time Uzbekistan and its neighbors were the center of the world. Until Vasco de Gama discovered the sea route to India in 1498, Central Asia was the Silk Road connecting the trade of two great economic and cultural powers, China and the Ottoman Empire. It was Shangri-la, the land of dreams, the birthplace of civilization and the stomping ground of Tamerlane of Samarkand, Genghis Khan, and Atilla the Hun, who marched back and forth juggling empires and atrocities. The Silk Road blew away hundreds of years ago but it took Soviet occupation to really bury this part of the world in the sand.

We're on our way to Karakalpakstan, which you won't have heard of. It's an autonomous republic in the north of Uzbekistan. And the town that we're driving to, Muynak, is at the end of the road. It might as well be at the end of the earth. Muynak was once a thriving town with a large fishing fleet, nestled on the shores of the world's fourth largest inland sea. But those shores are now over 150 kilometers distant, and the sea itself has shrunk to 20 percent of its original size. Where there was water, there are saline flats on which no harvest will grow. Salt and pesticide blow into town from the desiccated seabed. The people and their fleet are stranded.

The biblical quality of the disaster in Muynak—the replacement of water and prosperity with drought and desert—is dryly acknowledged in a saying that has developed in the town: that God, having blessed the area with wondrous nature, fell out of love with the people and sent them Russian engineers instead. These engineers rerouted the Aral Sea's source rivers to service "white gold"—cotton production on a scale that only the Soviet Empire could conceive. The industries that rose alongside have now vanished, along with the Soviet Empire that imposed them.

Like a dog expecting a kick, Muynak is a town that hugs the ground. No building is higher than one story, except a long-closed cinema, which is two. If you could be bothered to kill yourself, you'd find nothing worth jumping off. Expectations, morale, motivation are all as low-lying as the architecture. It's tangible: you can see it in the faces of the men who sit in the street, watching boys drive the cattle out to graze. Given the poverty (and the government tariffs), one can understand why there are no cars, but there are hardly any bicycles either. I remember hearing in Havana that the week after the Soviet Union collapsed and Cuba's only source of oil disappeared, China sent three million bicycles on two container ships. No such initiative here.

And then there are the stranded skeletal remains of Muynak's fishing fleet. Under a bleached and breathless sky, the boats list, landlocked. It's their stillness that is so strange. You see their shapes, and your mind expects them to be floating, bobbing. Your ears expect to hear waves slapping against hulls. But these hulks, tattooed with Cyrillic names, are silent and frozen. Sand completes the surreal and counterintuitive scene, in the way that the shapes of the dunes provide an echo of waves and water.

But the best way to appreciate the scale of the catastrophe in Muynak is to undertake the drive to the distant Aral Sea: five hours in a 4 x 4, driving across what should be a seabed, should be under a hundred feet of water, but instead is dust and scrubs and reeds.

Fitting the dreamlike aspects of the landscape, I am told a story that belongs in a nightmare. It describes what was once an island in the Aral Sea, but is now somewhere in the salt flats. When surrounded by water, the island was the home for Soviet experiments with Anthrax and biological weapons. There are two versions of accounts about what happened next. The first, more optimistic, is that after the collapse of the Soviet Union, the Americans came, saw what was there, and cleared it up. The second is that the Americans came, saw what was there, and fled. Either way, according to the story: "You could walk to this island right now, except that any mutated life that survived the Russians and the Americans might walk right back with you . . ."

A new word had to be invented to convey what the Russian engineers had done to Muynak and other similarly mutilated parts of the "Stans." The word, picked up by Robert D. Kaplan in his book *The Ends of the Earth*, was "ecocide," as he described how no other great industrial civilization so entirely and systematically poisoned its land, air, water, and people. Forty percent of the agricultural land is endangered; 16 percent is an ecological crisis zone; 20 percent of the population lives in regions of environmental disaster; 30 percent of deaths may be related to environmental factors.

Standing among the carcasses of Muynak's fleet, ecocide seems as good a word as any.

Muynak's tragedy, inevitably, does not end here. The health service that was once the pride of the nation spiraled downward in parallel with the decay of its citizens' livelihood. This coupled with poverty created the perfect conditions for a Victorian nightmare to rear its head: consumption. Now, the region's world-beating statistics don't relate to the size of its inland sea, but to the prevalence of tuberculosis and its sinister cousin, multi-drug-resistant tuberculosis, or MDRTB.

Tuberculosis, or TB, is a nasty disease. It's a social disease, a disease of the poor. And a killer. One-third of the world's population is currently infected with tuberculosis bacteria, and although it kills three million people each year, most of us can park the bug under the watchful eye of our immune system. But compromised nutrition, crowded living, inadequate ventilation, and late diagnosis all combine to make the poor easy pickings. Having lost their income, water supply, main food source, and doctors, the people of Muynak were sitting ducks. It wasn't long before Muynak had one of the highest incidences of tuberculosis in the world.

A local nurse is taking us to visit one of her tuberculosis patients at home.

We follow the sandy road that once was the sea and pause by a huddle of weather-beaten shacks. As we get out of the car, simply breathing the air becomes a constant battle to clear your throat of salt and god knows what else. And less tangibly unsettling, there are no insects here. It occurs to me that I've never been to such a hot place with so few flies. Maybe they steer clear of journalists because the place gets enough bad press anyway, or maybe they've been killed off by stuff we can't see. Or maybe they've just pushed off, sick of the sore throats.

The cottage rises like a mound of mud from the dusty soil. It's as beaten and bent as its owner, who shuffles to meet us in her yard of sticks and sand. Gulshat looks seventy-five but is in fact twenty-five years younger and she clearly isn't sharing the chief of hospital's enthusiasm for local life. Her story goes like this: Gulshat once worked in the fishing factory, and her husband was a fisherman. They had a simple life, a good life, but then the sea dried up. And now Gulshat is a barely living testimony to the devastation that poverty, and tuberculosis, can cause. First her husband died of the disease. Then her two daughters died in quick succession, one just months after the other. Now she is sick with it for the third time.

Tuberculosis is typically spread by airborne matter, a cough or a sneeze, propelling the bacteria into the air. A person needs only to inhale a small number of these to be infected. Around the world someone catches TB every second. What follows is a trial of coughing, weight loss, and sickness.

We take a brief tour of the house, involuntarily holding our breath. Although there are small windows in the one-story building, they don't open because hinges are too expensive for Gulshat to afford, and the custom has always been to block out sunlight during the summer heat and the wind during the winter. Thus the bacteria, destroyed by five minutes in sunlight, is allowed to cultivate in the dark.

Our translator looks nervous and hovers near the open door, but curiosity gets the better of me and I'm drawn deep inside. And what I find is haunting: two empty rooms with threadbare carpets, a single photo of each dead daughter adorning the walls.

Back in the reception area Karin is in deep conversation with the local nurse. As we turn to wave goodbye she whispers to us sadly, "She probably has a strain of tuberculosis that is resistant to this treatment. We don't have the drugs here yet to fight this. It's likely she will die."

After Muynak, the bazaar in Nukus seems a cheerful place. There are stalls selling third-hand electrical goods, innumerable Soviet medals, and fizzy drinks that have an incandescent chemical color. One can also buy LEMON BARF!—the local washing powder, not to mention a wide selection of fine Uzbek shoes. The families that squat on blankets, displaying their goods, seem reasonably happy, chatting or taking turns to doze in the shade. Turkish pop and rap blares nearby. And the children are pleased to find foreigners, because it gives them the chance to try out their "hellos," with their faces poised to burst into astonished delight if you hello back.

Before I am too seduced by the emerging marketplace, I am dragged off to a chemist stall within the bazaar. Across its counters lie a tantalizing display of candy-colored TB drugs.

Normal tuberculosis can be cured, but it involves a strict drug regime over a period of six months, and for some of this the patient must also be hospitalized. If the drugs aren't taken properly or the course is interrupted, resistant strains emerge. The collapse of the health structure, the shame associated with the disease, and the impossible financial burden of leaving the work force to be hospitalized for treatment has led to people self-medicating and a booming trade in black-market drugs.

Today, we are told by the chemist, there's plenty of Kanamycin, an important drug in the cocktail to fight TB. But the other drugs aren't in stock. This means that the chemist's customers will dose themselves with Kanamycin until they feel a bit better or run out of money, or until the pharmacist runs out of supplies. Whatever the outcome, almost none will complete the course. So the bacteria survives and strengthens itself against Kanamycin. Soon there is a killer disease that next to no drugs can beat.

Asbestos is everywhere: in the corrugated roofs, and wrapped around the oil pipes that feed the Stalinist housing. Plenty of high-rises here but none that you'd care to step into. You can see the asbestos shredding and tearing in the wind, as people hang carpets outside to air.

It is here, in Nukus, that MSF is daring to do what few will contemplate in such a deprived setting. Rather than go on treating patients with drugs that don't work, MSF has set up a pilot program for the treatment of multi-drug-resistant tuberculosis. It is one of only a handful of its kind in the world.

Many would say multi-drug-resistant tuberculosis is too expensive to treat in this poverty-stricken area. Treatment is lengthy and expensive even by Western standards. And we are, after all, in the middle of the desert. But MSF doctors want to give these patients a chance and prove that, even in the middle of nowhere, lives should and can be saved.

But it's tough. Unlike normal TB, the multi-drug-resistant strain requires eighteen months of constant pill popping, half of which is spent in the hospital. Patients feel nauseous and risk going blind. And there's no guarantee they'll even pull through.

I'm standing in a room of the MDRTB clinic, where the most vulnerable cases are. Karin reminds us to keep our masks on at all times. It's easier than you think to forget.

Murat is thirty. Both his parents died of tuberculosis, and he supports a sister of nineteen and a brother of twelve. His legs are literally like sticks, and it's hard to imagine how they will ever properly function again. He has at least five open holes in his side where attempts have been made to puncture and drain the mucus from his lungs—a slightly unorthodox procedure received in another hospital. They're like thumbholes in his rib cage, suppurating and glistening with pus. He coughs for my camera, which forces out more of the greeny-yellow ooze, followed by a delayed hiss from the bellows of his lungs. Looking at this toxic liquid is like looking at enriched uranium, like looking at death. It would take a much smaller amount than this to cause infection.

But Murat, when he gathers enough breath to speak, insists he is much better. Now he can sit up. Now he can talk. The new treatment is working.

Farida, however, has had ten months of treatment, but there is little sign of improvement in the painfully thin young woman.

"In another two months we have a very difficult decision to make," says Karin. "You can't keep people on this sort of drug regime endlessly." Farida's father is a doctor, and there's an unspoken certainty that he infected her and her four brothers, and that he will one day take her place on the ward.

Another woman of quite stunning beauty looks as if she's about to fall backward into an abyss, and you will be the one to push her. So she stays absolutely still. She stares at me like an animal trying to deceive a predator, hoping that if she does not move for long enough, I may forget that she is there. Balanced on the lip of a chasm, her fingers shake uncontrollably.

Outside in the clinic grounds I am greeted by a different scene. Laughter echoes across the shaded yard, and the sound of singing drifts up from the undergrowth. A group of girls giggle and blush as I pass, and I am unsure whether they are flirting with my camera or the men who hover by the garden wall. For these patients now enjoying the outdoors, the future has promise. They have successfully completed the first phase of their treatment and are no longer contagious. The prospect of returning home is just around the corner.

On my last day, MSF treats me to a meal in Nukus. We eat at a restaurant open to the street. Cars bump along the dirt outside. We are served barbecued pork, chicken, and French fries, cooked by the ancestors of Koreans who were dumped here by Stalin. And we toast each other on contraband Russian beer and local vodka. No one is exempt from the toasts, particularly the guests, and no one is allowed half-full glasses of vodka.

The group is an international snapshot: Karin, from Sweden, whose grace and authority has everyone wishing they were sitting beside her; Christine, the financial administrator from Germany, for whom no detail is too small to escape; Dora and Oliver, both doctors, from the Slovak and Czech republics respectively; Winnie Wong, the psychiatric nurse from Hong Kong ("And no, I don't play ping-pong"); Vladimir, the logistician from El Salvador, who is like a Central American Brian Blessed, sporting a death's head tattoo, and is determined to order ever-more powerful drinks; Jesse, a lab technician newly arrived from Kenya, who sips his Pepsi, remaining for the moment on the edge of the vodka world.

"Everyone else drinks vodka," booms Vlado. "Even if they don't like it. After all, you can mix it with anything! Ice cream, beer, tea! Cheers!"

Later, maybe a drunken hour or two later, news comes through of an emergency at the hospital. Oliver, as medical team leader, disappears. We learn that a girl of seventeen, admitted less than a week ago, has died. The evening stops, and the intense sadness that hovers malignantly above this land returns.

Dora and Vladimir burst into tears. I'm sure being away from home, working for nine dollars a day, creates its own pressures. And perhaps alcohol is a factor too. But nothing really can diminish the connection they had with this girl. And this, despite the fact that they didn't truly know her. Despite the fact that 30 percent of their patients die, and she was admitted too late and too weak, and that their only communication with her was in basic Uzbek or pidgin Russian.

But rather than becoming immune to the suffering as the disease becomes immune to the medications, they cared. They wanted her to have her life.

I'm left alone with Christine, and our conversation drifts back inexorably to the missing sea. She has been to the new edge of the Aral Sea and describes almost hallucinating during the five-hour drive. "Microscopic salt crystals in the air catch the headlights of the jeep . . . you drive and drive and drive but the water still seems to recede into the distance."

I ask her: And what does it look like when you get there?

"It looks like the beginning of the world."

A forlorn-looking nurse takes a break from treating patients with multi-drug-resistant tuberculosis.

Nurses and a patient in a
hospital fighting against the
high incidence of tuberculosis.

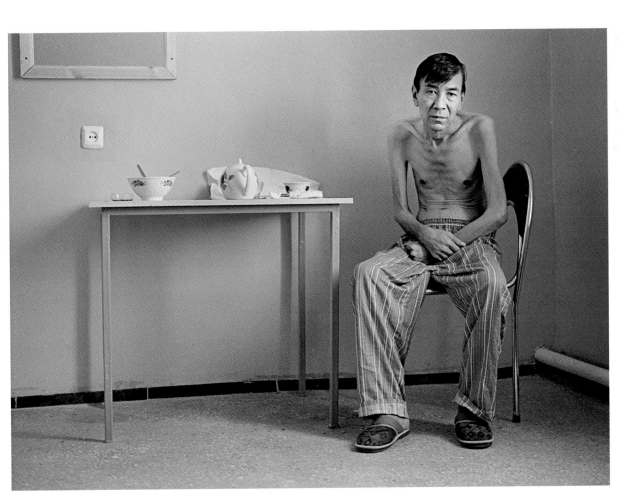

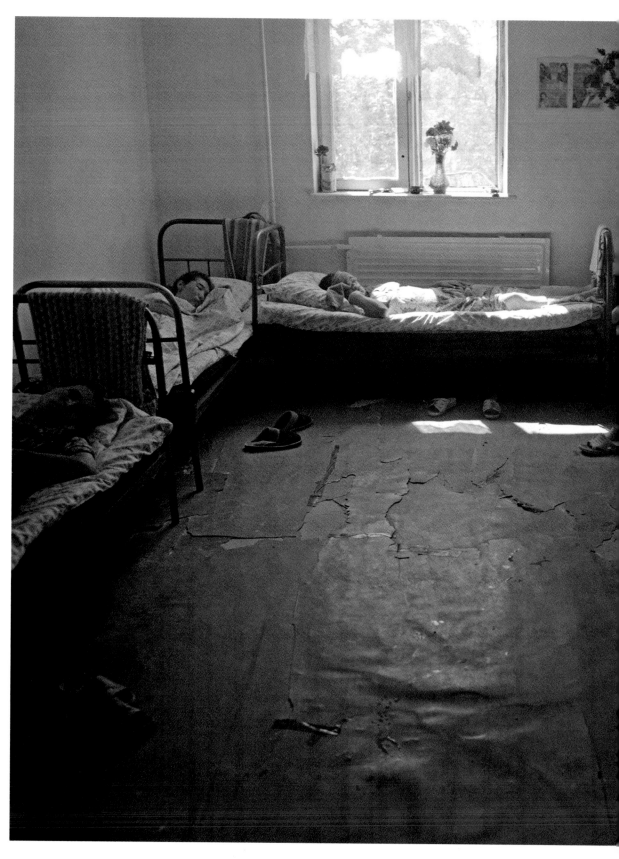

The hospital wards are full of tuberculosis patients.

Thirty-year-old Murat lost both his parents to tuberculosis and must support his brother and sister. It now seems he has the multi-drug-resistant TB, a vicious hybrid of a disease. Out the window is the toxic, broken landscape of Muynak, also riddled by an unflinching contamination. It's hard to imagine how either can recover.

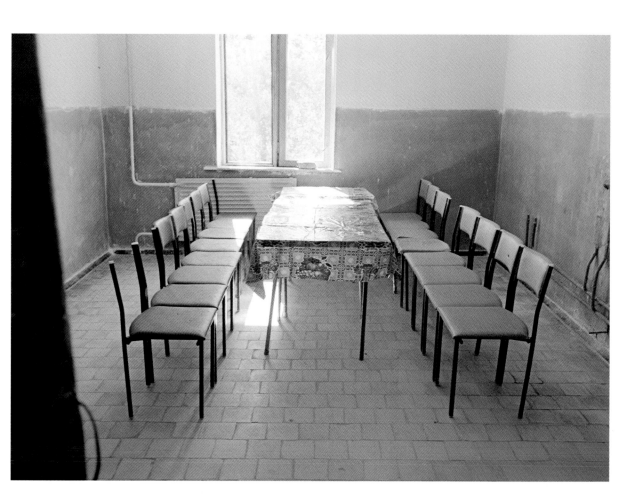

MARTIN AMIS published his first novel, *The Rachel Papers*, at the age of twenty-four. Following his award-winning debut with a string of stylistically complex novels, including *Money* (1984) and *Time's Arrow* (1991), he is widely regarded as one of Britain's leading literary figures, and an innovative postmodernist. In 2007 he was appointed as Professor of Creative Writing at Manchester University's Centre for New Writing, his first teaching post. His controversial writings about terrorism following the events of September 11, 2001, were collected in *The Second Plane* (2008). He lives in London.

DANNY BOYLE is an Academy Award–winning director and producer born in Radcliffe, Manchester, in 1956. After reinvigorating British cinema in the 1990s with the dark comedies *Shallow Grave* and *Trainspotting*, he entered the mainstream with his film adaptation of Alex Garland's *The Beach* (2001). Since then he has dabbled in different genres, including apocalyptic horror (with the box-office smash *28 Days Later*, 2002) and science fiction (*Sunshine*, 2007). His film *Slumdog Millionaire* (2008), which was filmed in Mumbai using a local cast and crew, won multiple prizes at the 2009 Academy Awards, Golden Globes, and BAFTAs.

TRACY CHEVALIER is a bestselling novelist whose works mix meticulously researched historical fact with compelling, imagined narratives. A graduate of the University of East Anglia's MA course in creative writing, she is best known for her second novel, *Girl With a Pearl Earring* (1999), a fictional meditation on the Vermeer painting of the same name, which was followed by a blockbuster film adaptation in 2003. Her 2010 novel *Remarkable Creatures* is based on the life of nineteenth-century fossil hunter Mary Anning. She lives in Hampstead, London, with her husband and son.

DANIEL DAY-LEWIS is an award-winning actor, renowned for his considered selection of roles and extreme dedication to his performances. After a youth spent in Greenwich and a period at Bristol's Old Vic Theatre School, he drew critical attention in 1985 with his performance in Stephen Frears's *My Beautiful Launderette*, and went on to star in such films as *The Last of the Mohicans*, *In the Name of the Father*, and Martin Scorsese's *The Age of Innocence*. He has received multiple awards throughout his career, and has twice won the Academy Award for best actor, including for his portrayal of deranged oil prospector Daniel Plainview in *There Will Be Blood* (2007).

MICHEL FABER's Dutch nationality belies the fact he has spent much of his life living elsewhere: he moved with his family to Australia in 1967 and has been settled in Scotland since 1992. His debut novel, *Under the Skin*, which mixes elements of science fiction with a sardonic literary sensibility, was published in 2000 and subsequently shortlisted for the Whitbread first novel award. In 2002, after twenty years of writing and research, he published *The Crimson Petal and the White*, a contemporary vision of the perversities of Victorian London, which became an instant bestseller. His book *The Fire Gospel* (2008) is a present-day reworking of the Prometheus myth.

JIM CRACE's fiction looks to new worlds, imaginatively reconfiguring the past and future to create odd perspectives on the present day. In 1986 he won the Whitbread prize for a first novel with his debut, *Continent*—seven short stories set on an imaginary new corner of the Earth. He repeated this success with *Quarantine* (a reimagining of Jesus' forty days in the desert), which won the 1997 award for best novel and was shortlisted for the Booker Prize. He is a member of the Royal Society for Literature and was awarded an honorary doctorate from the University of Central England in 2000.

DAMON GALGUT is best known for his novel *The Good Doctor*, which was shortlisted for the Man Booker Prize in 2003. Born in 1963 in Pretoria, South Africa, he published his first novel, *A Sinless Season*, at the age of seventeen. This was followed by *A Small Circle of Beings* (1988), a collection of short stories about his diagnosis of cancer at the age of six. His novel *The Impostor* (2008) won the University of Johannesburg Prize for creative writing, South Africa's second largest literary prize. He lives in Cape Town.

ADRIAN ANTHONY GILL is a journalist and critic whose acerbic views on travel, television, and food are among the most widely read in Britain. Born in Edinburgh, he moved to England as a small boy and studied at Central St. Martins and the Slade School of Art. Adopting his "AA Gill" byline to appear impartially androgynous for a piece in a friend's art magazine, he moved into first-person journalism at *Tatler* before joining *The Sunday Times*, his current home, in 1993. His columns have been collected in several books, including *AA Gill Is Away* (2003) and *Paper View* (2007).

JOANNE HARRIS worked as a schoolteacher for fifteen years while writing her first three novels. The third of these, *Chocolat* (1999), which was shortlisted for the Whitbread Novel of the Year Award, became an international bestseller upon publication and was adapted into an Academy Award–nominated movie in 2000. Her subsequent novels include *Coastliners* (2002) and *Runemarks* (2007), a fantasy book for young adults. She has also authored two cookbooks with Fran Warde: *The French Kitchen* and *The French Market*, and in 2004 published *Jigs and Reels*, a collection of short stories. She lives in Barnsley, fifteen miles from where she was born, with husband Kevin and daughter Anouchka.

HARI KUNZRU is an award-winning novelist and journalist based in Hackney, London. After graduating from Wadham College, Oxford, and studying for an MA in philosophy and literature at Warwick University, he contributed to various international publications, including *Wired*, *The Daily Telegraph*, and *Wallpaper**, where he was music editor from 1999 to 2004. In 1999 he was named *The Observer* young travel writer of the year. His debut novel, *The Impressionist*, won the 2003 Somerset Maugham award and was shortlisted for the Whitbread first novel prize. His third novel is *My Revolutions* (2007).

ALI SMITH's novels and short stories work with multiple perspectives, humorously and intelligently exploring notions of love, life, and sexuality. Born in Inverness in 1962, she read English at the University of Aberdeen before moving to Cambridge to study for a PhD. In 1995, after an unsatisfactory period lecturing at the University of Strathclyde, she published her first collection of short stories, *Free Love and Other Stories*, which won the Saltire Society Scottish First Book of the Year award. Her first novel, *Like*, was published in 1997, and her second, *Hotel World* (2001) was shortlisted for the Orange Prize for Fiction and the Man Booker Prize. Her 2005 novel, *The Accidental* (2004), won the Whitbread Novel of the Year Award.

JOHN MCGREGOR's first novel, *If Nobody Speaks of Remarkable Things* (2002), was composed when he was washing dishes at a vegetarian restaurant in Nottingham. It was a critical success, winning the Betty Trask and Somerset Maugham awards, and was shortlisted for the Man Booker Prize, making McGregor, then twenty-six, one of the youngest authors to be considered for the award. In 2006 he published his second novel, *So Many Ways to Begin*, which explores the history of Coventry through the eyes of a disillusioned museum curator. He lives in Nottingham with his wife, Alice.

DBC PIERRE was born in Australia, grew up in Mexico City, and now lives in Ireland with his girlfriend. At the age of forty-one, after years of concocting wild schemes and scams, he published his debut novel, *Vernon God Little* (2003), which won the Man Booker Prize and was adapted by Rufus Norris in 2007 for a celebrated production at London's Young Vic Theatre. In 2004 he appeared in *The Last Aztec*, a Channel 4 Documentary about the fall of the Aztec empire. His second novel, *Ludmilla's Broken English*, was published in 2007.

MINETTE WALTERS is a bestselling crime novelist whose works have been published in more than thirty-five countries worldwide. She won three major prizes for crime fiction with *The Ice House*, *The Sculptress*, and *The Scold's Bridle*, and has gone on to publish nine more novels, her latest being *The Chameleon's Shadow* (2007). Her first five novels have been adapted for television by the BBC, and her ninth, *Acid Row*, is in production with Company Pictures. She lives near Dorchester, Dorset, with her husband, Alec, and when not writing likes nothing better than pursuing her own DIY projects.

Acknowledgments

During the course of making this book there are a number of people I am indebted to for their energy, support, and professionalism. Petrana Nowill, whose tireless effort, determination, and enthusiasm were at the heart of the book. Every one of our incredible writers, who were brave and brilliant and who were the most remarkable and enlightening travel companions. Charles Miers for having the vision to make the book. Grainne Fox for her support. Bay Garnett for always being there. Hugo Grimwood for his constant work. Polly Markandya for seeing it through. Martyn Broughton and the team at MSF London. Polly Devlin for her help and Andy Garnett for his advice. Jean and John Lippet for their beautiful prints. Chris Ellis for his great work with the images. My family: Harry and Cath Craig and my sisters, Flora and Charlotte, who have always inspired me. Matt Willey for his passion for books and Dan Crowe for helping make it happen. Alex Tart for being calm in the storm. A.A. Gill for his much-appreciated support. Robin Morgan, Monica Allende, and Tom Reynolds, the team at *The Sunday Times* magazine. Frank Evers and Matt Shonfeld at The Institute for their professionalism. Alannah Weston, Kadee Robbins, and Minnie Weisz for being behind the work.

Last, but perhaps most important, every MSF doctor, nurse, logistician, driver, fixer, and translator who without exception gave up their beds to make space for us, drove us, fed us, propped us up, informed us, educated us, saved us, gave us the occasional much-needed beer, and inspired us all every step of the way.

— *Tom Craig*